# TAIJI FENCING PRINCIPLES, VOLUME 1
9 Foundational Principles For Applying the Daoist Sword Arts

# TAIJI FENCING PRINCIPLES

## Vol.1

by 夏崇义 Xia Chongyi

Daoist Sword Arts
Unionville, Pennsylvania

All rights reserved. This book or any portion thereof may not be reproduced or used in any manner whatsoever without the express written permission of the publisher except for the use of brief quotations in a book review or scholarly journal.

First Published 2017
Published by Lulu.com

Cover art by 裴理文 Joshua Paynter
Book design by 夏崇义 Chongyi Xia
Edited by Tyson Settle

ISBN 978-1-387-34346-1

Library of Congress Cataloging-in-Publication Data
Title: Taiji Fencing Principles, Vol. 1 / Xia Chongyi.
Names: Xia, Chongyi, author

COPYRIGHT © 2017 Xia, Chongyi

10 9 8 7 6 5 4 3 2 1

COVER PAINTING BY

裴理文
**JOSHUA PAYNTER**

**This book is dedicated to my master, Zhou Xuan Yun.**

Thank you for opening this gate for my life, providing me direction, community, and reason.

# FOREWARD

**Fencing with Xia**

It was during my first match with Swordsman Xia, while I was erratically changing time and distance, that and he paused the fight for a moment. And in that moment, he came close to me and said that if I'd like to continue fighting in the method of form and timing, we could. Or we could slow down, take a breath, and try something new. I decided to give his way a go. Instantly, I felt something more fulfilling. I could see things that I hadn't before: "If I go here, then that opens up there!" "If I maintain cohesion, I can still go this way." And of course the dreadful moments of seeing the cuts coming at me, abound. By no means was I close to winning. But the difference was that it didn't matter. Because I could see myself improving.

The second match with that same swordsman came about a year later. I found my adrenals firing up, almost the instant we crossed swords. And again, he stopped the match for a quick word, essentially saying the same thing he said to me the first time. We took a breath, crossed swords, and I suddenly found that everything fell away. It was just the swordsman and myself; and our swords. Suddenly, fencing became meditation, which became breathing, which became the moment. I can't say if it became the Dao, but it was close.

These moments provided clarity for me in my life after my father had recently passed away from cancer. My emotional life was in turmoil. And occasionally I wasn't sure if I was doing what I was supposed to be doing. I felt very lost. The Daoist Sword, in those moments, gave me a changed perspective on swordplay by enabling me to remain calm and breathe. The practice changed how I respond to life's struggles through the selfsame method. It is in this way that the method The Summer Swordsman teaches can truly be called the *Life-giving Sword*.

Swordsman Illingworth
Philadelphia, Pennsylvania

**Resurrecting the Art**

At some point, I realized that your sword methods are not about the movements, but about the core principles and philosophies. Structures of sinking the elbow and shoulder to join with the ribs while pointing the dantian towards the target. All the while, you're using taiji stepping, stillness, and calmness with sudden bursts; without fear or second guessing. There is a cohesion when dancing with a partner to match them through the yin and yang. Using core principles of the gates through softness and hardness with the angles of the body and the sword while reaching out through the tip. Manipulating intent, hiding it, dividing it, and directing it. And most importantly, letting go of things of the heart and soul such as ego, anger, hatred, to simply do and be. With that said, any movements of any style and weapon can utilize these principles.

Your life work in these sword arts is an amazing accomplishment. You defied a nation; an empire. The previous generations had tried to wipe out these arts, but you single handedly fought them all with an ideology. I hope the world can understand the significance.

**Swordsman Yuan**
**New York, New York**

*"The defining characteristics of the swordsman are Elegance & Uprightness."*

# Table of Contents

| | |
|---|---|
| Introduction | 21 |
| About Fencing | 26 |
| 9 Foundational Fencing Principles | 33 |
|   1. Structure & Alignment | 35 |
|     Body Alignment | 37 |
|     Alignment of the Front Foot | 46 |
|     Alignment to the Opponent | 50 |
|   2. Cutting the Hand | 55 |
|   3. Principle of the 8 Gates | 62 |
|     Inward & Outward Engagements | 63 |
|     The Eight Gates | 64 |
|   4. Controlling the Central Pillar | 96 |
|     Taking Control of the Central Pillar | 103 |
|     Maintaining the Central Pillar | 105 |
|     Regaining the Central Pillar | 106 |
|   5. The Swordsman's Hex | 111 |
|     Active Functions | 114 |
|     Passive Functions | 117 |

| | | |
|---|---|---|
| Applying the Sword | | 118 |
| Discussing Grabbing | | 121 |
| Locking the Sword | | 125 |
| Double-Locked Swords | | 126 |

**6. Dividing The Army** — **137**
Avoid Gambling — 139
Preventing a Divided Army — 140

**7. Controlling Initiative** — **145**
Taiji Theory for Initiative — 146
Harmony and Disharmony — 149
Four Phases of Momentum — 152
Relinquishing Initiative — 156

**8. Holding the Lines** — **162**
Extending though the Sword — 165
The Swordsman's Hex — 167
Cutting the Opponent's Changes — 169
Aligning for Cuts — 171
Threatening Lines — 172

**9. Three Types of Cohesion** — **177**

**Glossary** — **195**

# Table of Fencing Drills

Fencing Drill 1 – Maintaining Structure  53

Fencing Drill 2 – Maintaining Alignment  54

Fencing Drill 3 – Taking the Hand  60

Fencing Drill 4 – Changing Gates  94

Fencing Drill 5 – Central Pillar  109

Fencing Drill 6 – Swordsman's Hex  129

Fencing Drill 7 – Double-locking  132

Fencing Drill 8 – Dividing the Army  143

Fencing Drill 9 – Harmonious Swordplay  158

Fencing Drill 10 – Disharmonious Swordplay  160

Fencing Drill 11 – Holding the Lines  175

Fencing Drill 12 – Matching the Corporeal  185

Fencing Drill 13 – Matching the Energetic  187

Fencing Drill 14 – Matching the Strategic  190

Fencing Drill 15 – Balancing the Principles  193

# Introduction

The Daoist sword arts manuals presented here are a series focused on disseminating the tactic and methodologies applied in swordsmanship kept in the temples and communities of Daoism, and often times attributed to the masters from the holy Wudang Mountains. The sword fighting skills of the Daoists (both of Wudang and across China) were unique in that they could apply sensitivity, precision, and structure, instead of relying on swinging and blocking; hoping to have the correct timing and spacing alone.

These Daoist sword arts have been kept in manuals and dance rituals for hundreds–if not thousands–of years. But it is the goal of this book to somehow codify the tactics applied within these arts. This book is styled as a non-style specific study on body mechanics and the physics of two swords engaged in combat.

Presented here, in the first of four volumes, the Taiji Fencing Principles, Volume 1 offers the core material necessary for applying these sword methods. It is expected that by the end of this book, the up and coming swordsman should be able to feel comfortable in the engagement. The swordsman should overcome the confusion of the sword in their hand and better understand their opponent's cuts. After one's comprehension of these texts, they will have answers to many scenarios if given enough time. Through years of practice, the amount of time one needs to find a correct response will be reduced, and the swordsman will begin to move from a refined innate nature.

This volume focuses on the moments after the swords have been engaged. It may be assumed that the swords have touched because one sword is blocking or parrying the other, while it may be that both swordsmen fight from an engaged position. In either circumstance, these principles should always be tools available in the shortest and longest of situations. One's ability to react quickly and precisely will determine their skill level, and this may only be improved with practice.

Once these principles are comprehended and the skills are acquired, the second volume will introduce the idea of meeting swords and cuts.

It is important to consider the

differences between battling sword against sword, and sword against saber, as a curved edge and slicing style will present a different scenario. For the time being, we will focus on the straight sword engaged with another straight sword, for mutual practice and concept. Meeting a slicing sword will carry many similar skills in terms of applying principles, but the engagement will have differences in the way pressure is managed and timing.

It is very important to remember that all content in these volumes refers to two swordsmen engaged while holding a sword with only the right hand. When switching to both left-handed swordsmen, the art will be consistent, but reversed. When one swordsmen and left-handed and the other right-handed, a variety of principles from this book will not be applied the same way, and circumstances will be different. These topics will be covered in later volumes.

The future volumes in the Taiji Fencing Principles series will build on these skills as the primary tactics and terminology in understanding the engagement. Additional books in this Daoist Sword Arts series will include The Sword Virtue Studies, The Swordskill Studies, and The Sword Dancing Classic.

# About Fencing

Taiji fencing is both a fencing sport and a general training practice. The term itself refers to a fencing strategy revolving around an awareness of the balance of yin and yang energies in the sword exchange. Taiji fencing as a sport is a particular game used by groups to competitively swordfight, and test one's own skill under heightened pressures. But the general practice can also be considered a derivative of *tuijian*, or "pushing swords." Oftentimes likened to the practice in taijiquan known as *push hands (tui shou)*, pushing swords is a method of training one's movements while the blade is engaged in a parry or block with the opponent's sword. As the two swordsmen move back and forth looking for control and opportunities to attack, the blades seemingly never separate as their cuts and responses are so precisely timed.

    This is not to say that all taiji fencing requires the sword to stay in contact. Only in the introductory levels are the swordsmen required to maintain physical cohesion as a method of developing skill. As each swordsman progresses in their studies, the practice of pushing swords evolves gradually into free-fencing and free-fighting. One can see taiji fencing as a path to competent swordplay for students, both new and experienced.

This type of swordplay is said to be of a high level, and requires a great deal of refinement and practice. But because the purpose of this style is to **not get cut** and it is not designed to **get the better cut**, it offers a look at swordsmanship as a defensive and responsive art, not a chaotic exchange of steel and luck. Because one should pre-meditatively understand themselves and their mechanics, the opponent and their mechanics, the physics of the sword-fight, and the correct changes in positions and engagements to maintain proper defense, the complexity of this art is limitless as one looks deeper and deeper into the principles and forms.

Taiji fencing also offers a way to pressure test one's art and skill. Just as sparring tests the skill of boxing and striking arts, and wrestling tests the quality of throwing and grappling arts, the practice of taiji fencing allows the swordsman to find the holes in their skill and in their training methods. With constant pressure testing and responsive skill training, the swordsman should begin to find the techniques of their forms and drills in the fencing, and begin to open up new ideas and interpretations for each posture and skill in their practice.

For those new to this fencing skill, it is important to start by moving slow and steady. Try to avoid jerky and snappy reactions in practice. It is better to get tapped lightly than to hurt your partner with force and momentum. The give-and-take creates the balance and those with great skill should attempt more difficult techniques, while those new to the practice should focus on the basics being presented by their instructor and in this book.

It is recommended that one begins and practices taiji fencing with wooden swords. These *mujian* are the classical practice weapon, coming right after swinging a simple stick. Students may wish to wear goggles, a mouth piece, and a light glove on their sword hand. But it not expected that those practicing these fencing methods should need large pads and armor. This training method considers both swordsmen unarmored, and any cut is considered potentially dangerous, in terms of maintaining a defensive mindset.

With a goal of perfected skill, technique should be the key component to one's success. One should not rely on the quality of their sword, their armor, their speed, or their power. In a true conflict, these excellent tools can compensate for a lack of skill, and enhance those techniques which have been cultivated.

As familiarity with one's partner improves, their speed, power, and comfort with getting struck by your mujian will develop. As two swordsmen build a bond together through practicing, they will build a comfort zone where they may increase their intensity and quality of cultivation with a mutual level of understanding.

It is also important to consider that one should have an instructor when undertaking these skills. There are many great sword masters and teachers in the world. Finding one that embraces correct cultivation is a true treasure, and each instructor will provide unique keys to your development.

# 9 Foundational Fencing Principles

The 9 Foundational Fencing Principles refer to the first nine guidelines taught to successfully apply taiji sword skills in combat. This collection of ideas has been pulled from various sword classics and personal experiences. These principles have also been pulled from a variety of internal sword styles. Be it from Wudang's Taiyi, Taiji, Bagua, or Xingyi swordplay methods, each of these will offer a new layer to one's understanding of fencing and swordplay.

These nine principles may seem arbitrary in their order, but they are structured for the order of application in the *learning experience*. Each new consideration will build off the previous, and help fill in the gaps where the earlier principles leave off. Practice of these skills with the fencing drills provided will give you and your partner the necessary tools to develop competence in your fencing and swordplay.

# 1. Structure & Alignment

The structure of the body is like the structure of a house or building. The world will press upon it with forces of wind, water, flooding, earthquakes, and a variety of other hazards. And as with these structures, the body must withstand a variety of external pressures. Because of this, Daoist sword methods apply a similar internal alignments from the open-handed arts to the sword practice.

This section has three primary points of consideration:

1– Body Alignment
2– Aligning the Front Foot
3– Alignment to the Opponent

This replicates the Daoist conception of the Three Treasures, the Three Realms, and the Three Dantians. You must align your physical self; your jing. You must align your effort and energy to appropriately wield the sword; your qi. And you must be aware of the changes and concepts in the circumstances with your partner; alignment of shen. Refining these three aspects of your swordsmanship skillset will cultivate the three treasures of Jing, Qi, & Shen as well.

# Body Alignment

The alignment of the inside of the body requires deep study into the internal martial arts. Here, we will discuss it in a brief overview in terms of wielding the sword. We have to remember that these structures adjust and change as needed, but the principle should be consistently applied in practice. a primary concern in combat arts is to minimize moments where your body structure is compromised. When your opponent compromises your structure, it is important to be aware of how to regain appropriate alignment. Through application of these 36 fencing principles, you will learn various methods to reacquire your internal alignment and overcome the opponent's.

The first consideration is Aligning the Knee and Toes. These should always be pointing in a similar direction (see figures 3.1.1-3). As the hip opens and closes, the knee and ankle move together from the groin. Avoid rotating the foot to open the hips.

It is also important to remember that the weight should sit in the heel, not ride on the toes. Looking down at your foot, you will not only feel the difference, but you should see your toes beyond your front knees (see figures 3.1.4-5) Your hips should feel seated as if you are searching for a chair behind you to rest on (see figures 3.1.6-8). Your stance should only go as low as comfortable without causing tension in the back or an excessive forward lean (see figures 3.1.9-10).

Head should be lifted as it opens the back of the neck. There should be no pinching feeling in the neck vertebrae (see

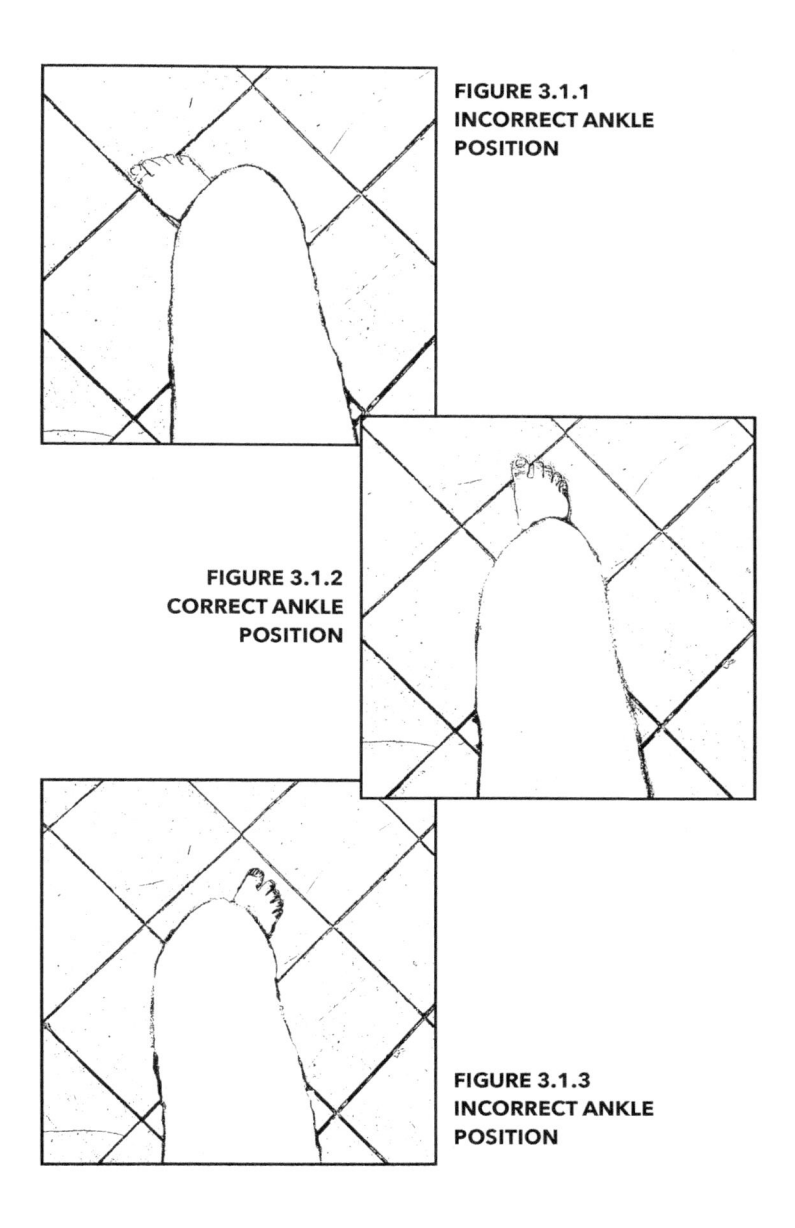

FIGURE 3.1.1
INCORRECT ANKLE
POSITION

FIGURE 3.1.2
CORRECT ANKLE
POSITION

FIGURE 3.1.3
INCORRECT ANKLE
POSITION

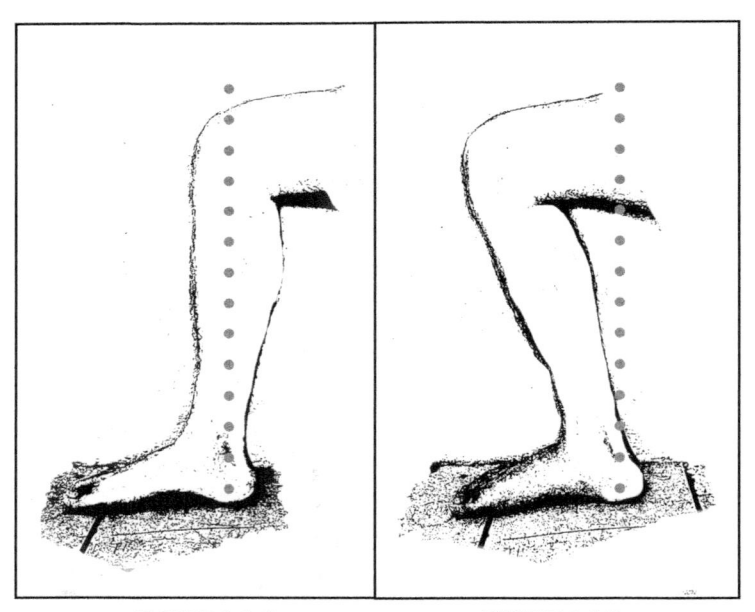

**FIGURE 3.1.4**
**CORRECT PLACEMENT OF WEIGHT IN THE FOOT**

**FIGURE 3.1.5**
**INCORRECT PLACEMENT OF WEIGHT IN THE FOOT**

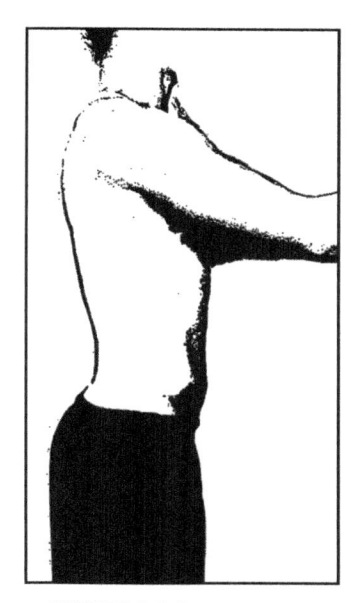

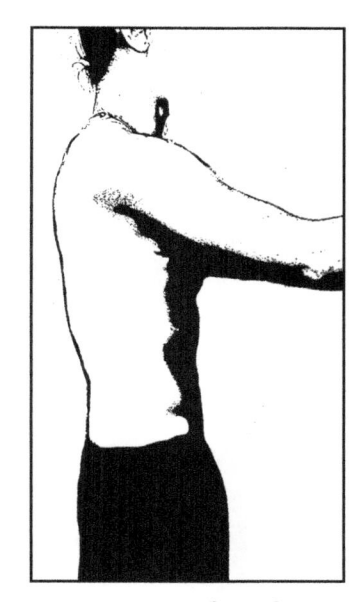

FIGURE 3.1.6
NATURAL
ALIGNMENT
OF THE HIPS

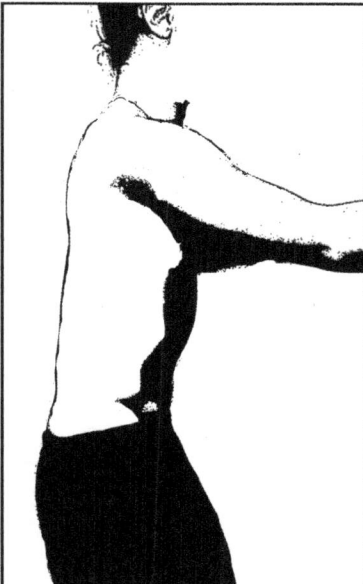

FIGURE 3.1.7
INCORRECT
ALIGNMENT
OF THE HIPS

FIGURE 3.1.8
CORRECT
ALIGNMENT
OF THE HIPS

**FIGURE 3.1.9 CORRECT SPINAL ALIGNMENT**

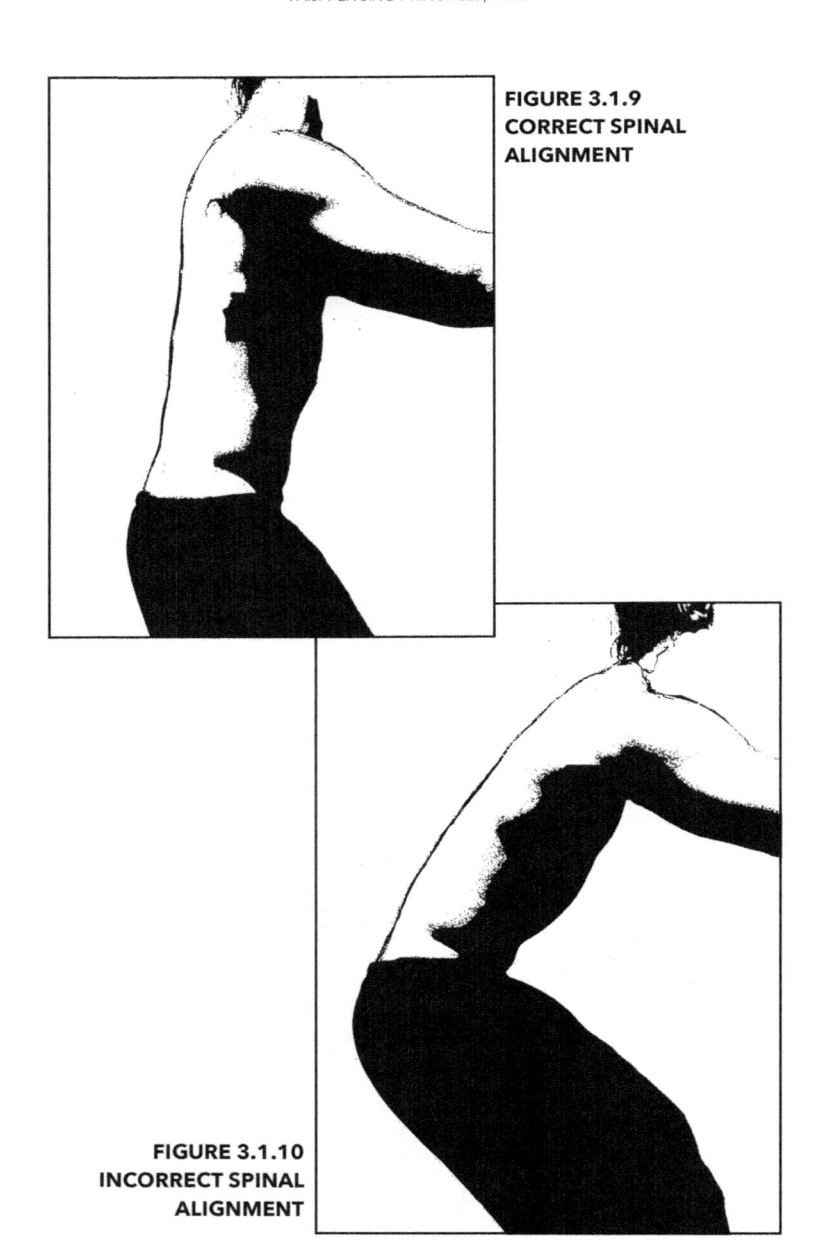

**FIGURE 3.1.10 INCORRECT SPINAL ALIGNMENT**

figures 3.1.11-12). This feeling stretches and extends down the spine as the tailbone opens the lower vertebrae between the kidneys. The hips may feel as if they are behind the feet and the heart.

This alignment does not require the swordsman to have a spine completely vertical the entire practice. As the head reaches up and the tailbone reaches down, they can be at any matching angle, as long as the light pulling sensation is consistent, in both directions.

The shoulder blades should be open in the back (see figure 3.1.13-15). The shoulders should feel sunken and forward, but the chest should then expand in the available space, without compromising the forward intent of the shoulders and shoulder-blades. Because of this positioning, any pressure received in the arms will be sent down the back to the hips

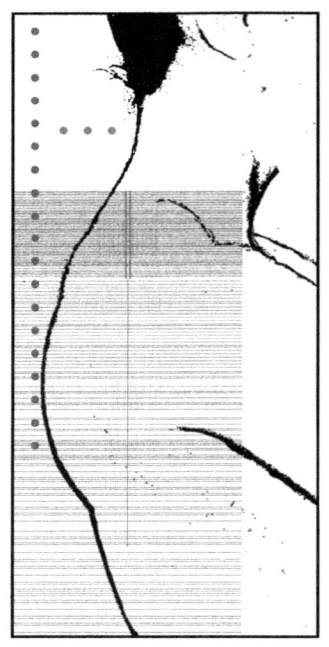

**FIGURE 3.1.11**
**HEAD RESTING FORWARD**

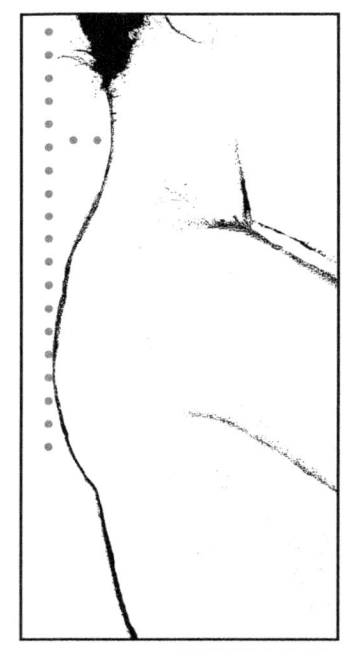

**FIGURE 3.1.12**
**HEAD LIFTED BY A STRING**

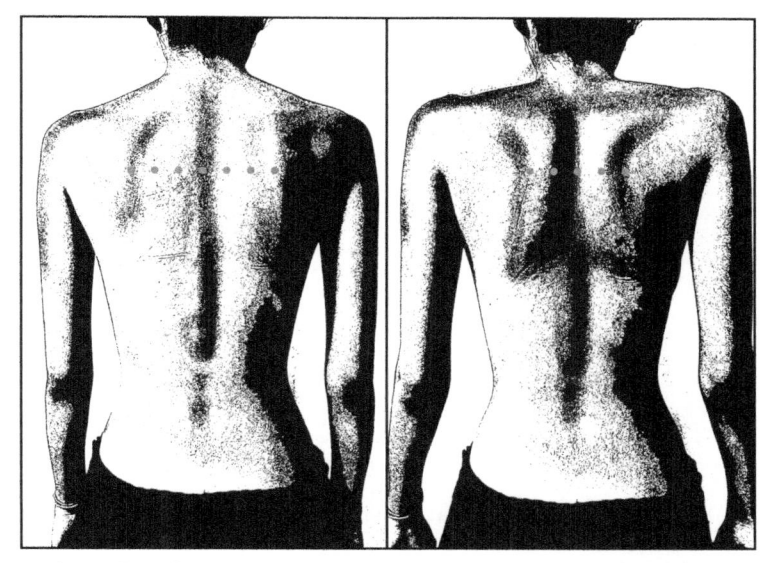

**FIGURE 3.1.13**
**NATURAL SHOULDER BLADES**

**FIGURE 3.1.14**
**PINCHED SHOULDER BLADES**

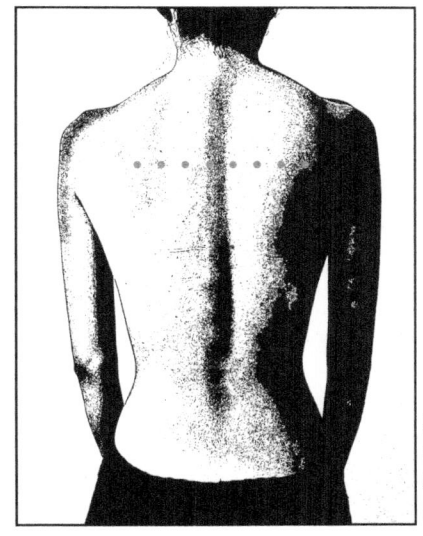

**FIGURE 3.1.15**
**OPENED SHOULDER BLADES**

and then to the heels and earth.

The elbows should be forward, down, and have maneuverability from the outside position to the middle-line (see figure 3.1.16-18). The elbow should be open as a larger **zhanzhuang** meditation type position (see figures 3.1.19-21). Because the swords cannot grab one another, this extended position is competent at receiving pressure. In swordplay one does not rely on defending against a pulling force like a smaller frame would protect from in the empty-handed arts.

## ALIGNMENT OF THE FRONT FOOT

It is important to remember that swordsmanship is a full-body art. Unlike some sport fencing methods, the Daoist methods utilizing both hands and three-

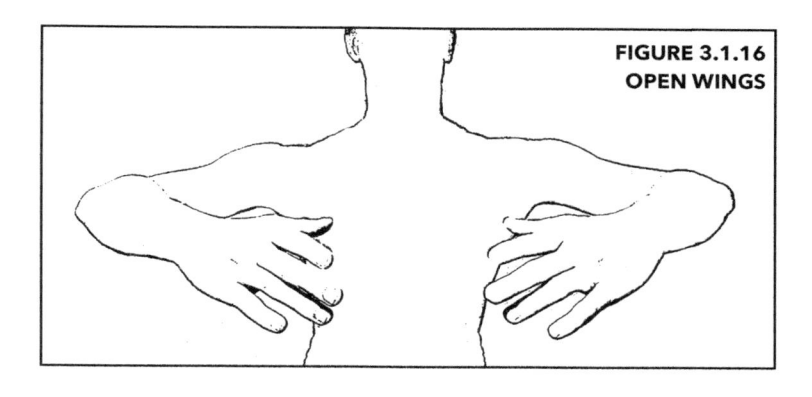

**FIGURE 3.1.16 OPEN WINGS**

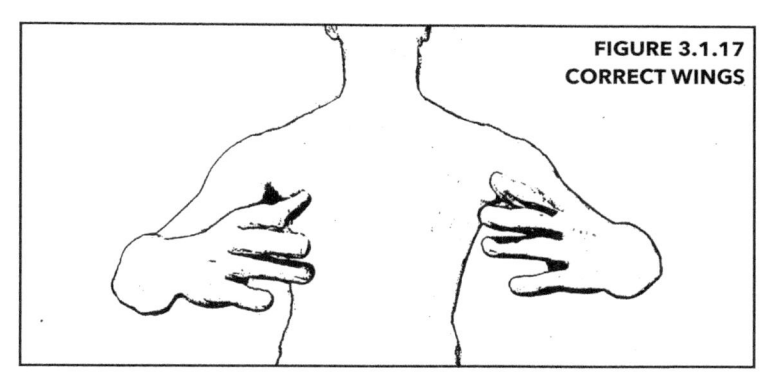

**FIGURE 3.1.17 CORRECT WINGS**

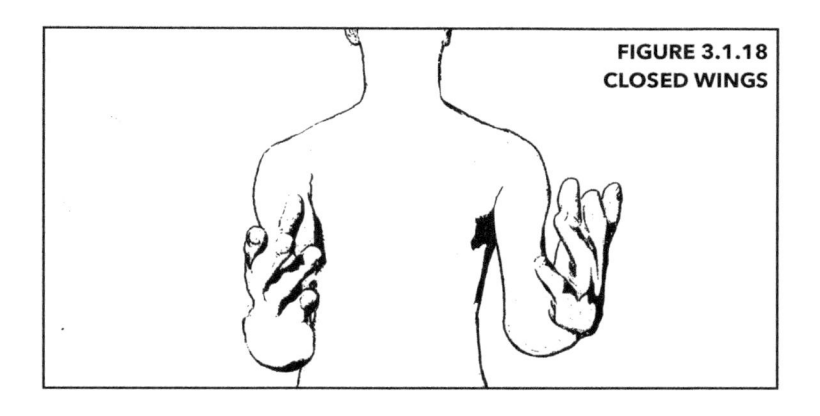

**FIGURE 3.1.18 CLOSED WINGS**

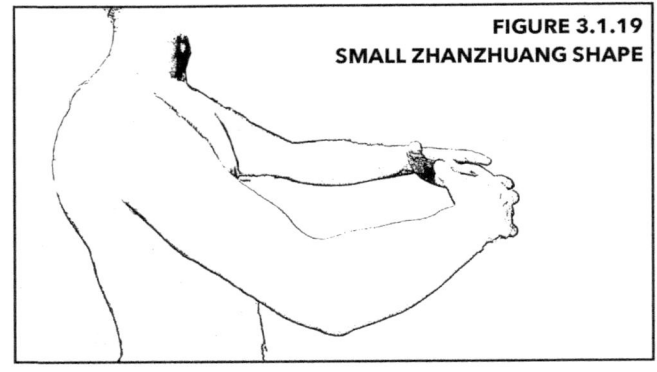

**FIGURE 3.1.19
SMALL ZHANZHUANG SHAPE**

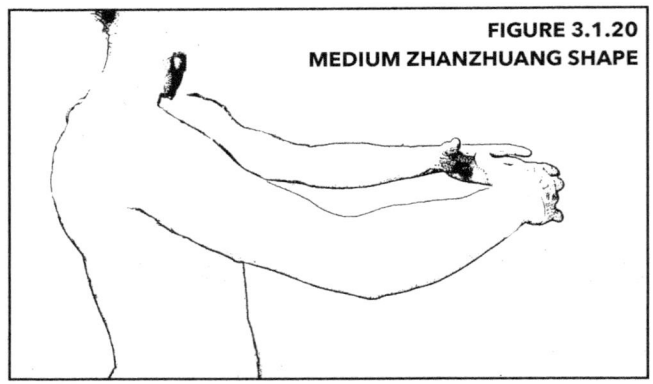

**FIGURE 3.1.20
MEDIUM ZHANZHUANG SHAPE**

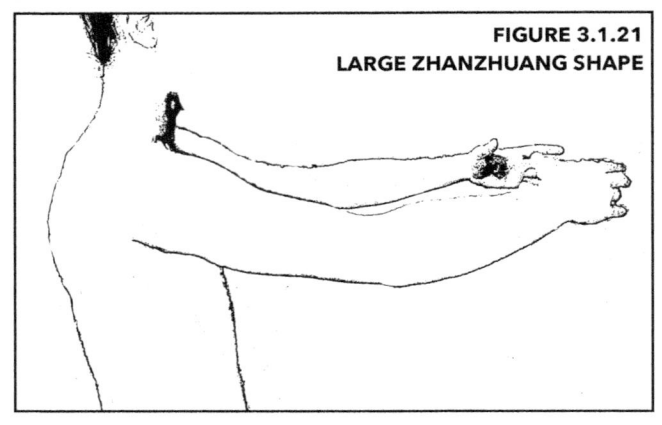

**FIGURE 3.1.21
LARGE ZHANZHUANG SHAPE**

dimensional stepping movements. Because of this, it is encouraged that one maintains a relationship between the front toe and the opponent. Our goal is not to fight sideways, but to cut off their angles with our body movements. Keeping your front toe towards the opponent keeps them in front of you, and allows you to have full range of movement of your sword and sword arm.

    One's ability to twist at the waist will allow for more movement variety without compromising the front leg alignment. Keeping the opponent in front of you, while you work to flank them and attack from their back will greatly rely on your ability to not let them get behind you. By turning your front foot inwards and away from the opponent, they already have a significantly shorter distance to cover to get behind you. Because of this, it is always important to keep your front foot always pointing towards the opponent.

## Alignment to the Opponent

In training, there is a saying that,

*"if you are looking down the line of the opponent's blade, you are already dead."*

What this means, is that the sword is so swift in real combat, that once you are in a straight line with the opponents blade, your life is entirely in the opponent's hands. The speed of a jabbing pierce is generally faster than ones ability to react with a parry or a dodge. Therefore, it is important to always be aware of where the opponent's sword is pointing, and always avoid standing directly in it's line. The opponent's sword should never be pointing at you. Through your own footwork, and your manipulation of your sword in contact with the opponents, you can avoid standing in the line of their thrusts and jabs.

When someone points a finger at you, the energy is felt, and the intention has a disruptive force. This sensation is emphasized when it's with a knife, a gun, a wooden sword, or a live blade. When a sword is pointing at someone, the initial and instinctive reaction is to flinch and press ones own blade against the infringing sword to redirect it's alignment. It is important to utilize this function with your own sword to help reduce how much effort the opponent is putting into pointing their sword at you.

In regards to the cultivation of the character of the swordsman, this exercise develops one's ability to control the opponent's attacks, and demonstrate superior skill before anyone is cut. Always being appropriately aligned will ideally leave the opponent with no opportunities to physically attack. If one cannot stop the fight through diplomacy, and one cannot run away from the situation, then demonstrating superior skill can prevent the combat from escalating by giving the opponent a chance to reconsider their involvement in the whole engagement.

# Fencing Drill 1 – Maintaining Structure

Both partners face one another with swords crossed in a forward position. The two partners should then slowly press on each other, gradually offering slow steps and changes of sword position to give a constant pressure to their own and their partner's internal structure. As you push on one another, the goal is to feel the pressure move past the wrist, shoulder, back, and hips, and go down into the heel(s). Both partners are looking for a constant sense of relaxation while there is a constant push on the structures due to correct alignment.

This drill can be done taking turns or simultaneously.

THIS IS NOT A SPARRING EXERCISE.

# Fencing Drill 2 – Maintaining Alignment

Both partners face one another with swords crossed in the forward position. With very, very, very little pressure between the swords, both partners work to stay out of the line of their opponent's sword, while the secondary goal is to keep the opponent in their own alignment. The free movement of the feet and body around the sword will be developed in later exercises also. But the goal here is to stay consistently out of alignment from your opponent's sword, while you are constantly keeping your sword pointed at them.

THIS IS A SPARRING EXERCISE WITHOUT ANY ATTACKS OR STRIKES.

# 2. Cutting the Hand

When two swordsman are aligned to duel, it is important to always consider the closest targets the opponent provides with you. When your opponent is cutting, this means their hand will be closest. The idea of cutting the hand also is the most peaceful martial response to physical aggression. By cutting the hand, you hope to disarm the opponent, rendering them unable to continue their pursuit. Here, they will be forced to reconsider the earlier opportunities to back down and stop the conflict.

Cutting the hand also address the concept of "meeting blades." This term refers to how you deal with the opponent's pressure. There are two types of pressure one can apply through the sword– momentum based, and structural base. In our style, we often avoid momentum based attacks as they reduce our ability to constantly change and adjust. Structural based power on the other hand does not have the speed to take advantage of the many short windows of opportunity for an attack. Because of this, we work on finding our own balance between these two, through fencing with our partners.

As equal blades cross in the middle positions, the controller of the force will be the one that presses on the other's sword harder. This battle of strength is to the advantage of the larger swordsman, but can also be utilized by all swordsmen with appropriate angles and adjustments.

If one wishes to reduce the opponent's force pressing on their structure, and increase one's own pressure on the opponent, it is opportune to bring the trunk of your sword closer to the stem of theirs. The negative trade off here is that you are bringing them closer to their target; your hand. The same can be true when reversed for the opponent.

This principle states that the closer your sword's tip get to their hand, the more control you give up, and the stronger their defense becomes. Finding the correct timing to close that space on the hand and void their cuts requires an investment of time in practice. Balancing momentum based speed with structural adjustments will be key to finding the hand before their cut finds yours.

Cutting the hand is also a way to teach your partner that they are being too static in their movements. A timely response is necessary in swordplay, whether you are moving at a slow or fast pace. In all circumstances, one should respond promptly and with impeccable timing. When an opponent becomes too focused on a particular strategy or pattern, the hand cut will come easily to their opponent. When someone becomes very pushy, it should be considered an opportunity to cut their hand, instead of stressing over their overwhelming force.

Remember that even after landing the hand cut, the swordsman must re-engage the opponent's blade to prevent the counter-cut. Cutting the opponent's hand may or may not end the fight, depending on the quality of the cut. But in the case that the attack landed was only superficial, the swordsman should be maintaining a constant defense, and not expecting the fight to be over after making contact. In an actual exchange, the opponent may not even realize they have been cut until their body begins malfunctioning due to severed muscles, tissues, or blood loss. Because of this, never allow your guard to drop, and never take a cut if it requires you to sacrifice your defense.

# Fencing Drill 3 – Taking the Hand

Both partners face one another in a forward position with swords crossed in either the front or back sides. It will be important to practice both.

The two partners will start stationary, and work on tapping each other on the hand slowly with control and steadiness. As the two swords circle and press on one another, the goal is to not escalate your response with flinching reactions. Stay calm, and look for the right movements of both the hand, and the tip of the sword, simultaneously.

As the drill continues, the swordsmen can begin moving their feet and circling one another to add another layer of distancing to the practice. But neither should attempt to attack other targets.

It is extremely important to develop good sword-hand defense. The initial cut (once blades make contact) will most often be a slide down the blade to the hand.

THIS IS A SPARRING EXERCISE WITH LIGHT CONTACT TO THE SWORD HAND ONLY.

# 3. Principle of the 8 Gates

When engaged with the opponent, the swords can point in various directions and meet at many different angles. There are a variety of benefits when pushing inward or outward. This will all depend on how the swords meet. The Eight Gates is a tool with which one can better comprehend the spacing and alignment of the weapons, and to better understand one's options in each of the various positions of engagement.

By studying the Eight Gates, one can begin to understand the shortcomings and advantages of each position. By learning to move between the gates both offensively and defensively, one can begin to control the battlefield and the opponent's actions.

## **Inward & Outward Engagements**

Once the swords make contact, the direction, force, and alignment of the swords and swordsmen will define the options available for both staying safe and finding opportunities to attack the opponent. To better understand these scenarios, we will discuss The Eight Gates.

When the swords are crossed (right-handed versus right-handed), the two blades can be in either the inward-pushing or outward-pushing position to one another. Outward-pushing engagement position refers to when both swordsmen are pushing outward on each other's blades (see figure 3.3.1). Inward-pushing engagement position refers to when both swordsmen have their swords pressing inward against one another's blades (see figure 3.3.2). These two positions will constantly be changing depending on how one moves through the Eight Gates.

## **The Eight Gates**

The Baguatu, or the Eight Trigram Diagram, is a tool in Daoist arts such as geomancy, astrology, and divination. This map places eight symbols around the Taijitu

**FIGURE 3.3.1 OUTWARD ENGAGEMENT**

**FIGURE 3.3.2 INWARD ENGAGEMENT**

(Symbol of the relationship between yin & yang) in varying arrangements. Each arrangement offers different values, and can be used to better understand the process of change and reaction.

The Eight Gates in Taiji Fencing correlate directly to the Baguatu. In this version of the diagram, the trigrams are organized based on the relationship between the swords, and how one can adjust and move with the opponent.

To describe each of the eight gates, we will assign them trigrams. As in the Bagua, the eight trigrams are the Heaven, Earth, Fire, Water, Thunder, Wind, Lake & Mountain. It is important to remember that in this fencing system, the trigrams for one person will not be the same for the opponent. When the opponent's trigram is considered with ones own, then you will form a corresponding hexagram, aligning with those in the Yijing, generally.

When discussing the Bagua, we first will give a label to each of the three lines for each trigram. The bottom line will be called the Foundation Line. This line will be discussed first, as all things build from the foundation (or root).

## FOUNDATION LINE

When discussing the Eight Gates of Taiji Fencing, the Foundation Line refers to whether the sword is pointing to Heaven or Earth. When the tip of the sword is above the handle (pointing at least 1° upward), then the Foundational Line is considered Yang; represented by a solid line. When the pommel is more upward, with the tip—even in the slightest—towards Earth, then the line is split; considering it Yin. When the sword changes between pointing upward and downward, the Foundational Line is considered the Changing Line

See figures 3.3.3-4 for examples of the Yin and Yang positions of the Foundation Line.

**FIGURE 3.3.3
YANG FOUNDATION POSITION**

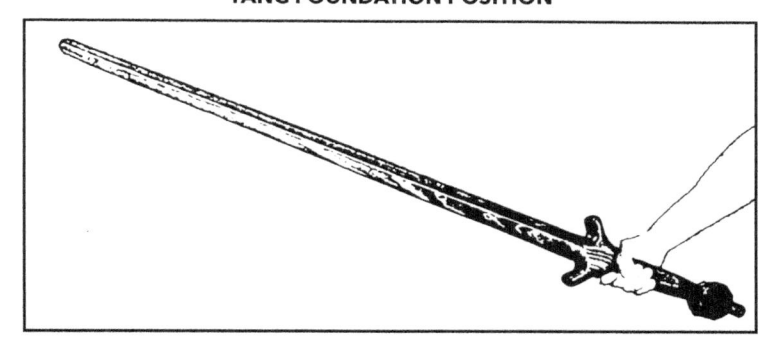

**FIGURE 3.3.4
YIN FOUNDATION POSITION**

## BREATH LINE

The Middle line we will label the Breath Line. Referring to the Chest cavity, and to Heart (Middle) Dantian. Just as the Foundation Line has a Yin and Yang position, same is true with the Breath Line.

When the two swords are crossed, you form an alignment between the two swordsman's center lines with the sword somewhere between the two. When the swords are moved to the outside position for the swordsman, then this is considered a Yang Breath Line. This means that the movement of closing the chest would bring the sword towards the opponent. You are in the more open position, relating the shoulder to the opponent.

Inversely, when the swords are crossed, and moved to the inward direction for the swordsman's shoulder, the swords should move to the left of the line between the two swordsman, and the opponent may seem slightly behind the swordsman, or to the outside. This is the Yin position, with the shoulder in a more closed alignment than when the swords are to the right of the central alignment.

Because this has no relationship to whether the contact of the swords is to Inside or Outside, we call the Yang position Open and the Yin position Closed. Changing between the left or the right of the center of the swordsman will determine whether the Breath (middle) Line is Yin or Yang.

See figures 3.3.5-6 to see examples of the Yin and Yang positions of the Breath Line.

**FIGURE 3.3.5**
**YANG BREATH POSITION**

**FIGURE 3.3.6**
**YIN BREATH POSITION**

## INTENTION LINE

Once the Foundation Line at the bottom, and the Breath Line in the middle are both understood, we can now address the top line; the Intention Line. The intention Line refers to the relationship between the swordsmen in consideration to who is controlling whose sword. Obviously, both positions to be discuss are applicable in offense or defense.

The Yang Gate for the Intention Line is when the sword is on the outside position, pushing in towards the opponent and their blade. This is yang because it is forcing the opponent's sword to be between themselves and your blade. It is Yang because it is controlling the opponent's options. Your position may feel endangered as the opponent's sword may or may not have an open line of attack to you, but because they are pushing to prevent your cut, you are controlling their action, and limiting their ability to act on their own will.

Vise versa, When the sword has an open line to the opponent but is staying in contact to prevent the opponent's cut, this is considered the Yin position. From the Yin position, you may be able to disengage to cut the opponent, but you are also giving up your own defense when taking a cut from this Gate (without appropriate footwork).

See figures 3.3.7-10 for examples of the Yin and Yang Positions of the Intention Line.

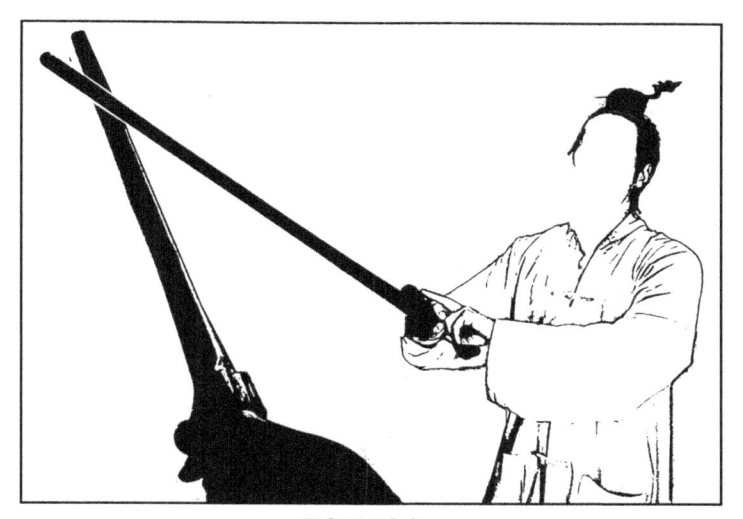

**FIGURE 3.3.7**
**POV IN YANG INTENT POSITION**
**FIGURE IN YIN INTENT POSITION**

**FIGURE 3.3.8**
**POV IN YIN INTENT POSITION**
**FIGURE IN YANG INTENT POSITION**

TAIJI FENCING PRINCIPLES, VOL. 1

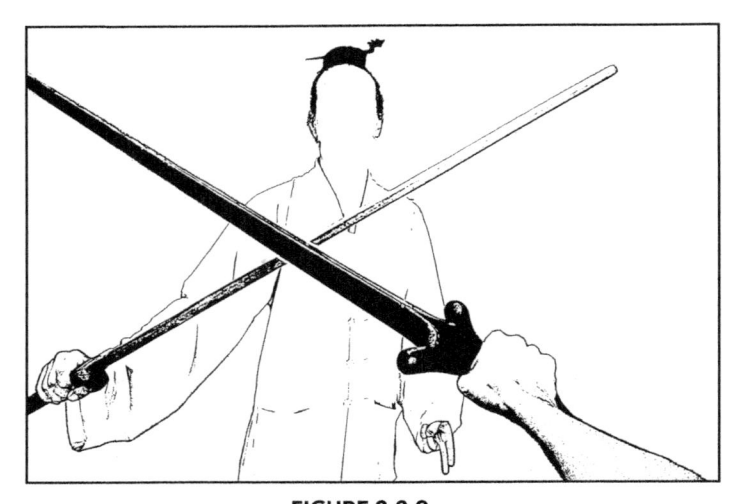

**FIGURE 3.3.9**
**POV IN YANG INTENT POSITION**
**FIGURE IN YANG INTENT POSITION**

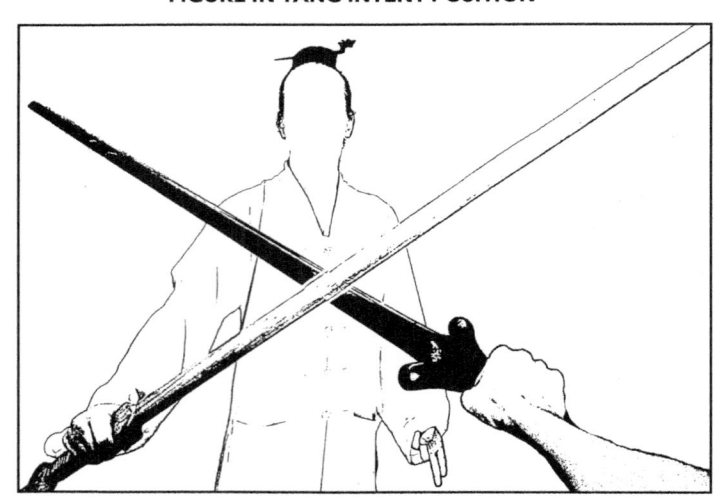

**FIGURE 3.3.10**
**POV IN YIN INTENT POSITION**
**FIGURE IN YIN INTENT POSITION**

## Eight Trigram Diagram

Now you have been introduced to the each line for each of the trigrams. Their positions and relationships with one another can now be discussed. Figure 3.3.11 shows the alignment of the Eight Trigrams in the Bagua used in discussion of the Eight Gates. As a reminder, the orientation of the Bagua and the placement of the trigrams comes in many variations. The most famous are the Pre-Heaven and Post-Heaven arrangements. This one is specific to these fencing methods.

As depicted in the figure 3.3.11, the Bagua is not aligned with the Trigrams directly up and down; left and right. Instead, it is tilted 45 degrees so you have two trigrams in each of the four corners.

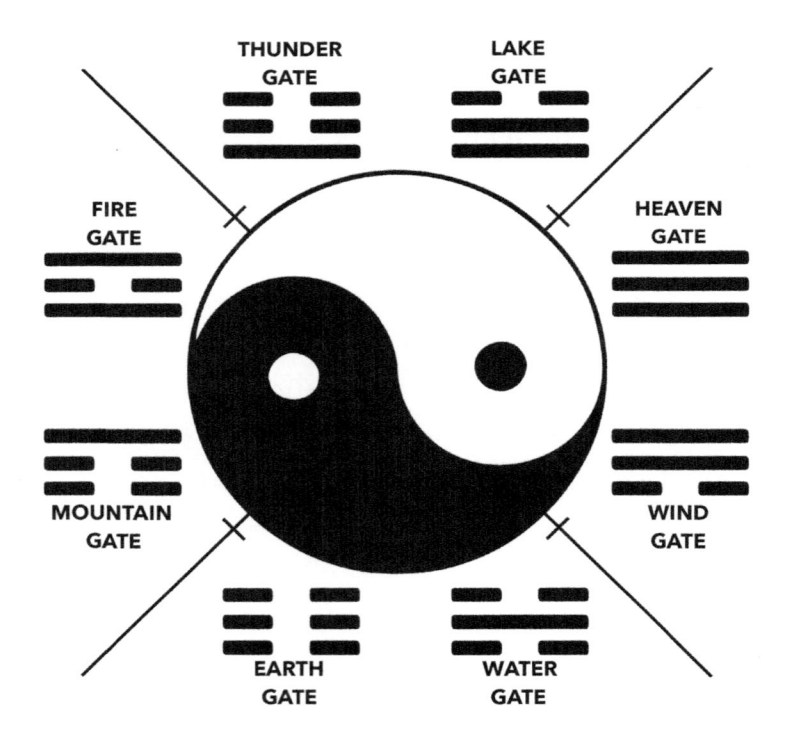

**FIGURE 3.3.11
EIGHT GATES BAGUA**

## The Trigrams

When the swords are pointing upward, and crossed with your chest open, you will be in either the Lake Gate—if your Intention Line is Yin (see figure 3.3.12)—or in the Heaven Gate (see figure 3.3.13), if your Intention Line is Yang.

**FIGURE 3.3.12
POV IN LAKE GATE**

**FIGURE 3.3.13
POV IN HEAVEN GATE**

Applying this same principle, when the swords are pointing up to the left position (with the sword in the right hand), you may be in either the Fire (see figure 3.3.14) or the Thunder Gate (see figure 3.3.15). Once again, this will be determined by your sword being on the inside or outside position with the opponent's sword.

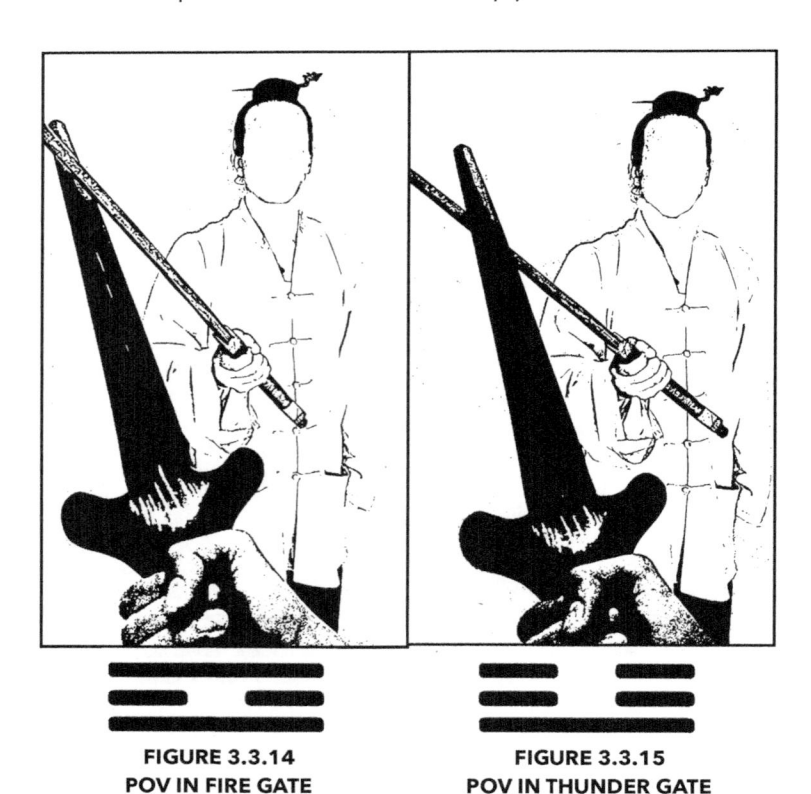

**FIGURE 3.3.14**
**POV IN FIRE GATE**

**FIGURE 3.3.15**
**POV IN THUNDER GATE**

As we follow the circle that is between you and your opponent, as your sword points downward and across, you now have found Mountain Gate (figure 3.3.16) when the sword is pressing towards the opponent, and the Earth Gate when your sword is between the opponent and their blade (3.3.17).

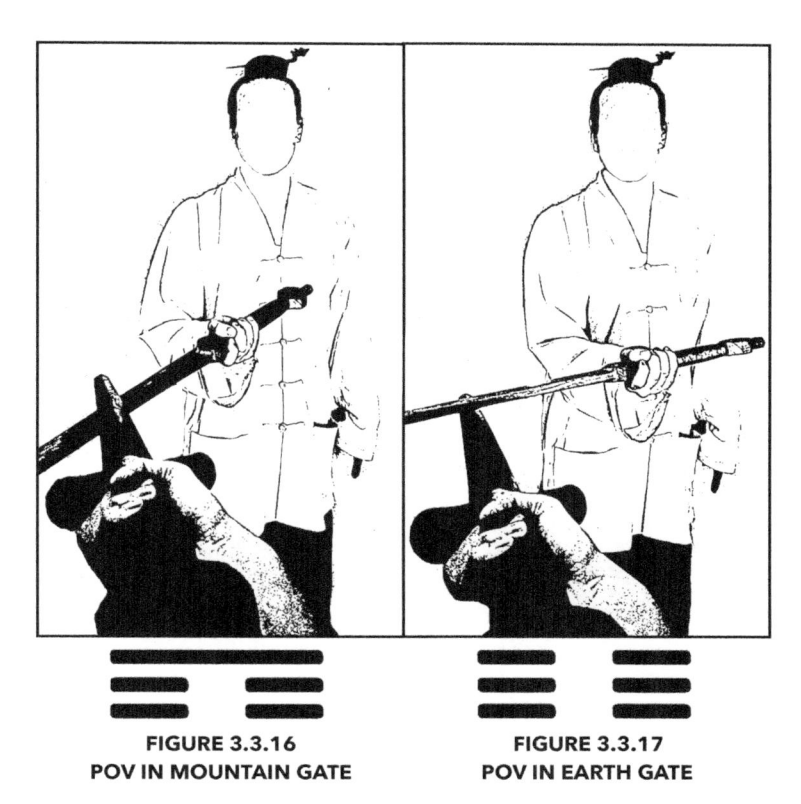

**FIGURE 3.3.16**
**POV IN MOUNTAIN GATE**

**FIGURE 3.3.17**
**POV IN EARTH GATE**

The final pair of gates will be to the bottom right corner, and these are the Water and Wind Gates to the downward-right diagonals. In this direction, your sword will be in the inside position when in the Water Gate (see figure 3.3.18), and on the outside position when in the Wind Gate (3.3.19).

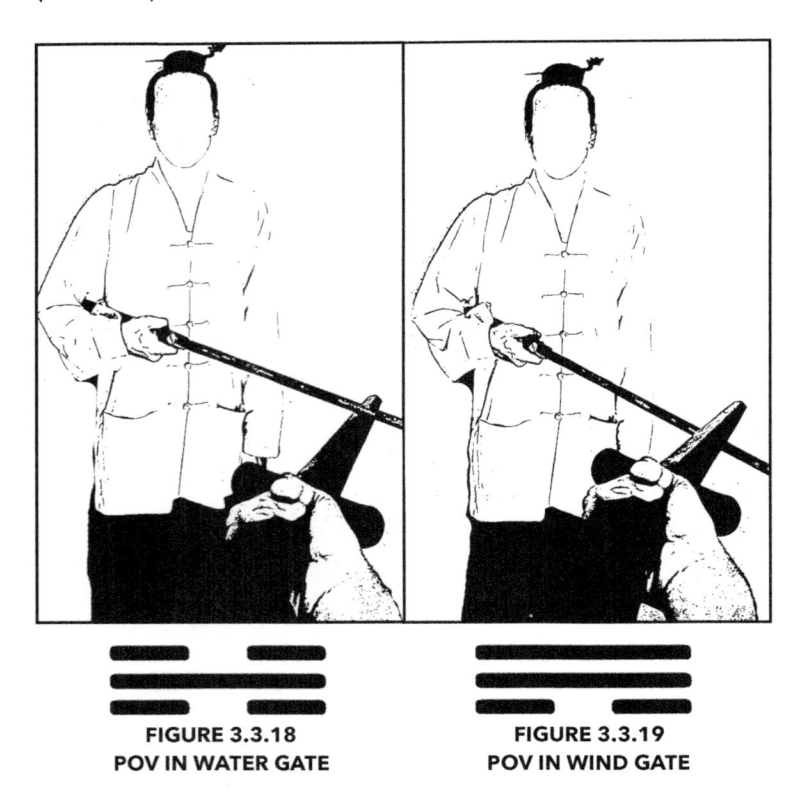

**FIGURE 3.3.18**
**POV IN WATER GATE**

**FIGURE 3.3.19**
**POV IN WIND GATE**

Your ability to understand and visualize these eight positions, will determine your ability to understand the transition of the sword. As the lines change, different relationships will appear and disappear. Additionally, the opponent's gates and changes will not always correspond to yours as foot work and the alignment of the two swordsmen will determine what is most opportune in the moment.

## Changing Gates

After studying Figure 3.3.11, you will need to cross swords and see how one can change between the different gates. There are many methods to moving from any of the Eight Gates to any of the the others. It is important to work through each gate with a variety of methods to understand the options.

Here are a few important principles when discussing how to change between gates:

## Changing the Intention Line by Changing Foundation Line

When changing the Foundation Line, if the swords do not disengage, you will also change the Intention Line.

This means that when the opponent is defending your cut from your Yang Intention Trigram Gates, you can change your Foundation Line to cause your Intention Line to change to Yin. This works when changing the Foundation Line to or from Yin or Yang. See figure 3.3.20-21 for examples.

**FIGURE 3.3.20
CHANGING FROM WIND TO LAKE GATE**

**FIGURE 3.3.21
CHANGING FROM FIRE TO EARTH GATE**

The reverse is also true. It is important to remember that footwork will also affect these changes.

## Changing the Intention Line by Changing the Breath Line

When changing the Breath Line, if the swords do not disengage, you will also change the Intention Line.

This means that when the opponent is defending your cut from your Yang Intention Trigram Gates, you can change your Breath Line to cause your Intention Line to change to Yin. This works when changing the Breath Line to or from Yin or Yang. See figure 3.3.22-23 for examples.

The reverse is also true. It is important to remember that footwork will also affect these changes.

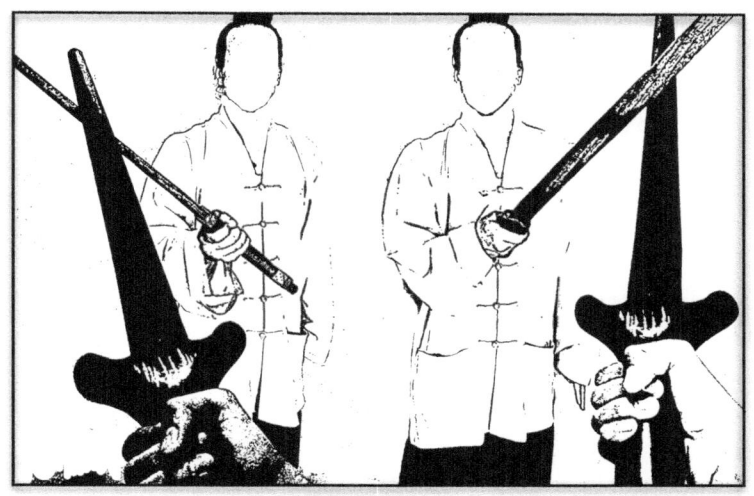

**FIGURE 3.3.22**
**CHANGING THUNDER WIND TO HEAVEN GATE**

**FIGURE 3.3.23**
**CHANGING FROM EARTH TO WATER GATE**

## Stirring to Change the Intention Line

When pressure is light, and the opponent is not active, one may use a stir of the tip of the sword to change to the inside or outside of the opponent's swords. This affectively changes the Intention Line either Yin or Yang.

## The Cycle of Changes When Engaged

If the two swords are engaged and do not disconnect, one can see how the eight gates transform from one to the next. If you and your partner line up with the swords in your Heaven Gate (pointing the swords upward, to the right corner, with your sword on the outside), one can drop the sword down the right side to enter the Water Gate. Here, without disengaging, one has changed the Foundation Line yin, and this has caused the Intention Line to also transform to Yin.

Moving across the legs without disengaging, the Breath line of the Water gate becomes Yin, while the Intention line also transforms into Yang, becoming the Mountain Trigram.

Now on the bottom-left-outside position, When raising the sword up the left side, you actively are changing the Foundation line back to Yang while maintaining a Yin Breath Line. Because you are changing the Foundation line, you are also changing the Intention Line back to Yin, placing you in the Thunder Trigram.

Thunder will follow all the previous logic as you open to the right and change the Breath Gate Yang, maintaining a Yang Foundation Gate, and allowing the Intention Gate to Change as a response to

Yang. You have now returned to the Heaven Gate.

Once you are familiar with this cycle, you will want to go the opposite direction through the same Gates. Once you are familiar going in both cycles, you are then encouraged to place the swords in an Inside position to one another, and move through the other four gates. The order will be: Lake to Wind, Wind to Earth, Earth to Fire, Fire back to Lake. The other direction will have a reversed order.

## Defending the Gate Change by Changing Twice

When the opponent leads you to change either the Breath Line or the Foundation Line, while you are in the Yin Intention Line Gates, you may be susceptible to their cuts as they reposition and enter the Yin Intention Line Gates themselves, and place you on the outside (Yang) position. To counter this, it is important to change a second gate simultaneously. If they move the swords from pointing upward to downward, you should bring them across the body. If they push the swords across, you may press them up or down to change the gate a second time simultaneously.

By causing two gates to change, you practically negate their initial attempt to change the Intention Line for both of you. Practically— because there may be a moment of opportunity depending on the footwork and alignment of the swordsmen at the time.

### **Sinking & Rising, Strafing Side-to-Side**

If you do not wish to allow your opponent to change the Intention Line by manipulating the Gates through changes in the Foundation and Breath Lines, you have the option also to respond by sinking and rising or moving sideways.

When the opponent wishes to move from a Yang Foundation Line to a Yin in order to take the Yin Intention Line Position, one option is to drop the body to the earth, lowering the sword fight, and no longer requiring your sword's tip to drop downward. Likewise, when you have the swords pointing downward, you may choose to raise the handle above the head in order to keep a Yin Foundation Gate and prevent them from taking the Yin Intention Line position from you.

The same principles apply when discussing defending changes in the Breath Line, with the difference in the type of response. Instead of going up and down with the sword, when the opponent pushes side to side, you can also move with the swords to keep your Gate. By side stepping and circling the opponent as they apply force, you retain your gates and find or lose opportunities to make a cut.

# Fencing Drill 4 – Changing Gates

Both partners face one another in a forward position with swords crossed in either the front or back sides (Inside Position or Outside Engagement). It will be important to practice both.

The initial exercise will not require one to attack the hand, but instead will focus on the shoulders (emulating the head) and the front knee. Keeping the swords engaged, the two swordsmen will press the swords through the gate changes in attempt to find a clean cut from one of the four gates with the Yin Intention Line.

Once both partners get the hang of this idea of changing the Intention Line between Yin and Yang in order to have an unobstructed cut and prevent being cut, then the swordsman can add back in the previous drills so the swordsmen also attack the hand. This will help break up the predictability between movements, and can be used to disrupt the partner's momentum.

As the drill continues, the swordsmen can begin moving their feet and circling one another to add another layer of distancing to the practice. But neither should attempt to attack any targets other than the knee/leg, hand/arm, shoulder/head.

**THIS IS A SPARRING EXERCISE WITH LIGHT CONTACT TO THE SWORD HAND, FRONT LEG, AND SHOULDER/HEAD AREA.** It is important to be clear the level of contact and targets you are allowed to touch with the sword. Having mutual balance is important when finding a partner one can trust in sword training.

# 4. Controlling the Central Pillar

The action of controlling the **central pillar** is the method one applies to maintain correct positioning in regards to the opponent. In the circular arts, the Central Pillar is considered the point of contact between the two combatants. When two swordsmen cross their blades in combat, the point of contact is what we call the **point of engagement** (see figure 3.4.1). If one were to draw a line from the earth below the point of engagement, directly up through it into the sky, this would be a line tracing the central pillar. A constant awareness and ability to manipulate the alignment of the swordsmen in relationship to this place in space will play a significant role in determining which techniques one

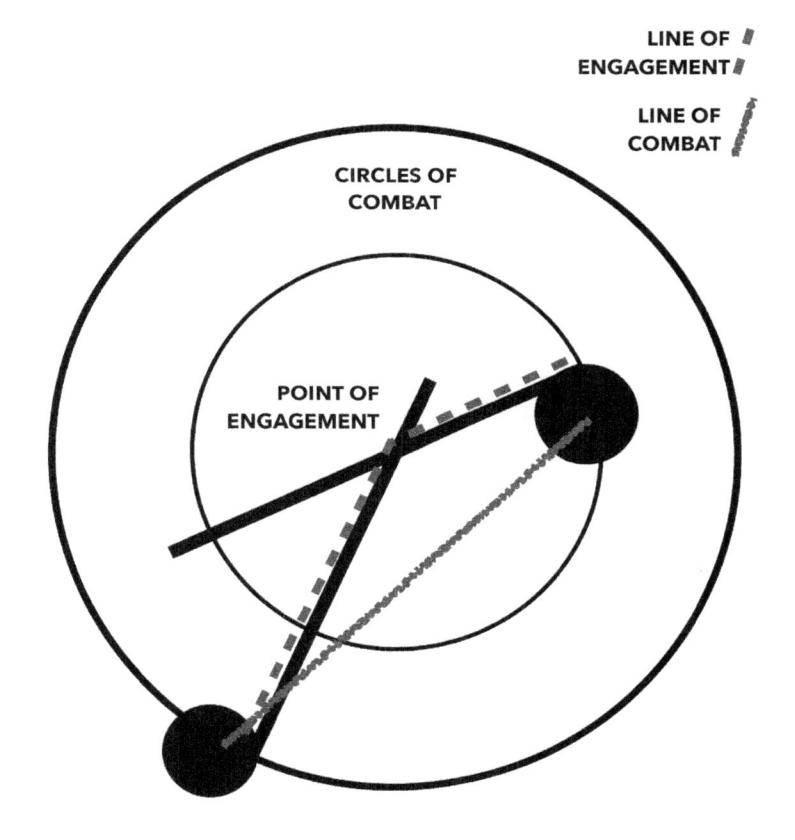

**FIGURE 3.4.1**
**OVERVIEW OF THE ENGAGEMENT**

has available to them, and what intentions one can develop.

When both swordsmen are pushing against one another's blades, they are in affect trying to control the **circle of engagement**. The circle of engagement can be visualized as the space surrounding the point of engagement, with the swordsmen on the circumference of the circle(s). Although the swordsmen are not consistently on opposite poles of the circle, the circle moves w/ the swords, with the maximum size being when both swordsmen have their arms extended and only the stems of the swords crossing. The swordsmen can move themselves around the circle to change their alignment to the opponent, bend their arm or shift forward to bring themselves closer to the center, or can push the swords side to side to relocate the center of the circle of engagement.

In the scenario that both swordsmen are holding their swords in the right hand, and the swords are crossed directly in between the swordsmen in an outward engagement, then the central pillar is directly on the **line of combat** (pictured in figure 3.4.1). The line of combat is defined as the direct and shortest line between the two swordsmen once engaged. No matter where the swordsmen have their swords engaged (directly between them, pushing to either side; up or down), the line of combat will not change or bend from being directly between the two swordsmen. It can exist anywhere within the circle of engagement, but will always be the shortest distance between the swordsmen's center lines.

The line of combat meets with the swordsmen from either the front or the back. When the swordsman meets the Line of Combat from the front, this means the line going between their center and the opponent's comes from the front of the body, without the sword or sword arm obstructing the line. When it is said the line of combat meets the swordsman from the back, this means the line is drawn either directly to the back or sides of the swordsman, or their sword arm crosses the line of combat. This means that at no point can both swordsmen have the line of combat in front of them. Either one, the other, or both have the line to the back.

The practice of *controlling the central pillar* is the action used to keep the line of combat in the most opportune position for one's self. Proper manipulation of the central pillar can determine if the opponent is attacking you or fighting for position. Most often, the initial actions in an engagement are to fight and take control of the central pillar, and align one's front along the line of combat, while placing the line of combat to the back of the opponent.

When two swordsmen engage directly across from one another with their swords between them, then this means the swordsmen are on opposite poles of the circle of engagement and that they are engaged on the line of combat (see figure 3.4.2). Once either swordsman pushes the Point of Engagement to either side, the swords have now left the line of combat, and the Central Pillar has shifted with the **point of engagement**. Visually, the two swordsmen are now reaching in the same direction with their swords, but have no weapons between their bodies. The action of pushing the point of engagement outwardly, moving the central pillar to the right, places the line of combat in front of one's self, and to the outside the opponent's forward lines (see figure 3.4.3).

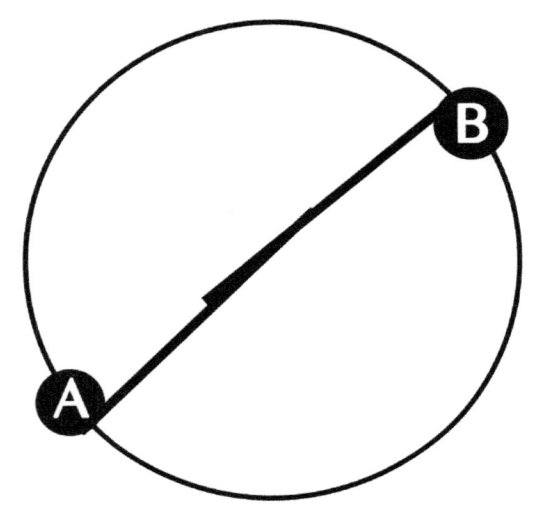

**FIGURE 3.4.2**
**ENGAGED ALONG THE LINE OF COMBAT**

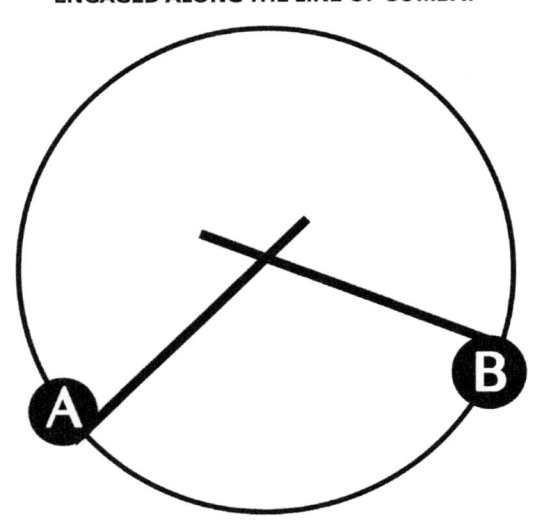

**FIGURE 3.4.3**
**B TAKES CONTROL OF THE CENTRAL PILLAR**

This is the ideal scenario for entering forward on your opponent. As you circle to the left, you maintain your position behind the opponent, while they fight to bring the swords back between you or move to their left in order to bring the central pillar back to the line of combat.

## Taking Control of the Central Pillar

There are multiple methods to take control of the Central Pillar from the Line of Combat. But it either requires being in a position to push outward, or causing the opponent to push inwards with force and momentum.

If one can hold the position in space with the sword, the movement of one's feet to the left can also take the pillar into one's front alignment, and get the back of the opponent.

It is recommended that one understands pushing outward with the tip to find alignment, then with the chest and shoulder blades to make the pressure. Angling the blade with the Wrist will find the correct alignment for creating the cohesion and potentially open the blades to the right of the Line of Combat at the first moment.

Opening from the legs and chest will then allow one to put the full force into the action. With correct stepping and rotation, one will find superior position right away.

## Maintaining the Central Pillar

Once you have the Central Pillar in front of you, your opponent will try various techniques to regain it. It is important to stay responsive with your stepping as you circle forward and to the left to close the distance. Your goal is to make your angles of attack as direct and forward towards your opponent as possible. Circling counter-clockwise will help evade your opponent's response of running forward, or around to your right.

It is important to prevent the opponent from changing the Foundation or Breath gate as well. If you are no longer pushing outward, you may no longer be able to apply pressure in the correct direction to keep the Line of Combat in front of you, and outside of their front alignment.

## Regaining the Central Pillar

If you have lost the Central Pillar, you will first need to decide if you will respond from an inward or outward engagement.

If using an inward pressure engagement, you will need to give them a target to chase as they cut inward, and allow them to bring the Central Pillar back to the Line of Combat. Once this happens, it is necessary to switch to an outward-pushing engagement to maintain control of the Central Pillar.

When in an outward-pushing engagement, you will have two primary options for bringing the engagement back to the Line of Combat or your front alignment. Choosing which of these will depend on available space, the size difference between the swordsmen (height and reach), and the energy in the moment.

If the swordsmen have room to maneuver, one may aggressively retreat directly down the Line of Combat away from the opponent. This will extend the space between the swordsmen, which will also gradually pull the Central Pillar back to the Line of Combat as well. There is no short cut for the pursuing opponent to take as you are traveling at a straight line in regards to them, not the swords or the environment. Take note, that a skillful opponent will be aware of your intentions and pursue you faster than you can retreat. Forward momentum has more speed and a quicker acceleration than retreating. Because of this, the retreat must be appropriately masked.

When space is not available, the swordsman will have to use the vertical circle to lift the swords up and over (or in the reversed scenario, jump over while pressing the swords down and across). Lifting the swords over head, the swordsman can freely move below the engagement, in effect, trading places with the swords.

This type of technique can be difficult for taller swordsmen against shorter swordsmen, but with good stances, it is applicable by everyone. Additionally, this skill requires a bit of risk, but offers a large reversal of circumstances with the opponent.

# Fencing Drill 5 – Central Pillar

The two swordsmen will engage with the swords crossed so that they foundation line is yang, and they are in an outward engagement. While pressing, the two swordsmen will move their feet to constantly work and keep the line of combat to the opponent's back, and maintain control of the central pillar. For this exercise, the focus is on positioning, not seizing or cutting.

In the case that the swords engage with an inward position, the swordsmen should try to change the foundational line to yin (pointing the swords downward) so that they are once again in an outward engagement, this time towards the legs.

Once this exercise is established, the two swordsmen will use the methods presented in this chapter to begin taking back and maintaining the central pillar. Once again, there should be only avoidance of the left hand's reach, and no actual grappling or snatching until correct movement is established.

# 5. The Swordsman's Hex

The left hand is often held in the position known as the Swordsman's Hex (see figure 3.5.1-2). Other common names for this Daoist mundra are: Sword Finger, Sword Hand, Secret Sword, Knife Hand, Hex Hand. The name has evolved as different instructors have discussed it's application in different settings.

In the Daoist community, this is a classic hand-posture used when a sword is

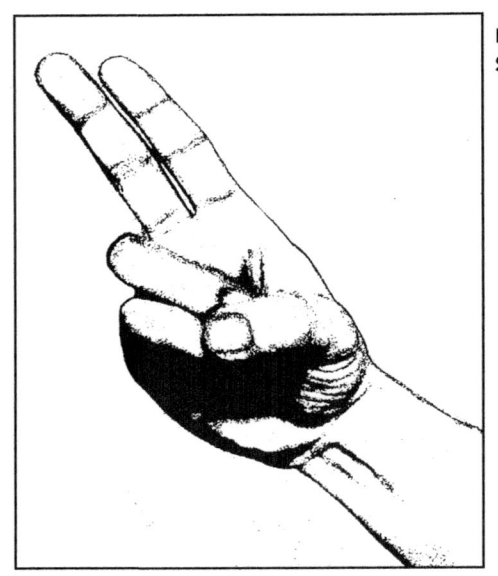

**FIGURE 3.5.1
SWORDSMAN'S HEX**

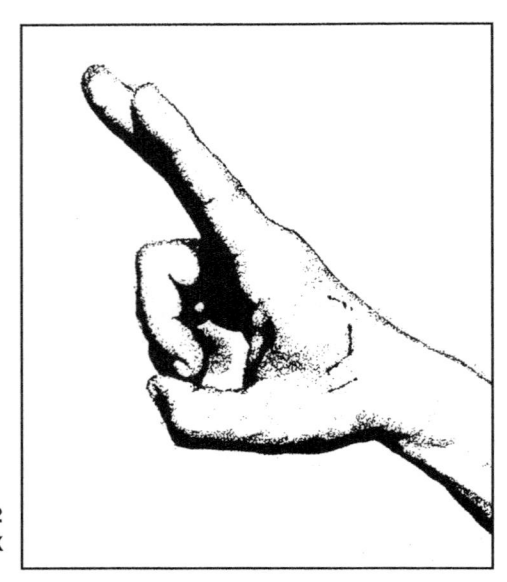

**FIGURE 3.5.2
SWORDSMAN'S HEX**

not available. Often times rituals will use the Swordsman's Hex when only using a sword implement for a short period, as well. Many times the priest will use the sword to cut away the ties, re-enact spiritual battles, hold spiritual fights, and to carve calligraphy into the material of the universe. Use of the sword finger can channel similar intentions, carrying more force than simply pointing, and activating particular muscle groups and vessels in the hand and arm.

In our practice, the Swordsman's Hex has 9 Active Functions, and 3 Passive Functions. These include: **Striking, Pressing, Grabbing, Splitting, Casting, Knife, Poking, Leading, & Throwing; Balancing, Holding, & Preparing.**

Active functions refer to the swordsman using the sword finger hand as the primary tool in the moment. These include different types of attacks and grabs.

Passive functions refer to a benefit given by practicing sword finger, even when it is not the focus of the technique or movement (defined often times by the use of the eyes).

## Active Functions

**Striking** – The Swordsman's Hex mundra can be used to represent any attack as it strikes the opponent as a palm, fist, or finger strike.

**Pressing (and pushing)** – Its movements may also encode how to parry the opponent's sword arm or body while dealing with yours and their cuts. May also double for pushes to attack the opponent's center.

**Grabbing** – The sword finger can be a representation of grabbing the opponent's weapon or arm to actively bring them in or around.

**Splitting (intention)** – Pointing the Swordsman's Hex at the opponent can bring a great deal of sudden intention and/or discomfort to an opponent. This may be a genuine attack or a faint to divert the opponent. Using this to distract will be it's own principle in the next chapter.

**Casting (spells)** – In a religious setting, the sword finger was used as a channeling tool for magic and rituals.

**Knife ( or off-handed weapon)** – Although you may not train with a dagger, this hand may be practicing the attacks as if wielding one while using the primary weapon to parry and engage the opponent's sword.

**Poking (pressure points)** – Knowing the softest and most vulnerable points on the body can be beneficial even for those that prefer striking methods to poking. Pressure point awareness provides focal points for training and visualization of technique.

**Leading (to maintain intention)** – When the sword moves to a rear position or the opponent circles to your left, the sword hand can provide a sense of threat while the sword recovers position.

**Throwing (weapons)** – Consider the swordsman's hex as more than attacking with the off hand, but also posture for having structure when throwing the weapon to a disengaged opponent.

## PASSIVE FUNCTIONS

**Balancing (the body)** – By activating the Swordsman's Hex, both sides of the chest cavity, thorax, torso, and waist are supported by active force. This maintains equality when training one handed weapons, and strengthens the whole technique in practice.

**Holding (the line)** – Discussed in detail later, this concept helps maintain position over your opponent, and regain position through structural force drawn from extending one's reach through the fingers.

**Preparing (the changes)** – Placement and momentum of the sword finger will provide balanced movement and align the body's mechanics for the upcoming changes one moves into and through. Understanding the placement of the left hand in the various scenarios will open different options of how to change with your opponent.

## APPLYING THE SWORD

There are many exercises one can develop when preparing for all of these circumstances. One of the primary considerations is to avoid bringing your sword or self in the reach of the opponent's Swordsman's Hex.

One should always consider the opponent's off hand as either armed or grabbing relentlessly.

Once again, you will find the previous principles build on this concept as you work to control the Central Pillar and to bring the opponent's sword arm into your own reach. Constantly attacking this arm and having two limbs to fight with will give you an advantage when circling behind your opponent.

When you view your postures from training your traditional sword form, it is important to look at the line of motion of the Swordsman's Hex and how it moves in relationship to the body and the sword. Which of the various active functions do you find for each change and posture?

It is simplest to begin with imagining or using a **Knife**. Watch the cuts you perform with the left hand, and consider them while your sword is engaged in the opponent's weapon. The knife should slip around the opponent's weapon, or attack their sword arm and front leg.

When the knife is forward and the sword is back, consider the threatening action, and reflect on the principle of

Leading as you use foot work to bring your sword back to the front and reengage.

    Consider the methods and ways of attacking the opponent's sword arm, to hold them at bay while you enter with your own sword. are you pressing their arm away, grabbing and holding it, or are you striking them while you make space for your own weapon to proceed?

## Discussing Grabbing

When grabbing the opponent's sword arm, there are more and less practical methods. These are the preferred grabs, depending on where one lands the left hand.

**Elbow/Forearm** – When meeting the opponent at the elbow, it is usually best to press the elbow into their body. This will help collapse their structure, and bring both swords closer to the opponent's head/torso/legs (see figure 3.5.3)

Grabbing at the elbow gives the opponent more control over you than you over them. Press or push whenever meeting this high up the arm.

**Wrist** – When meeting at their wrist, it is important to control where the wrist is in space in relationship to you. If you can grab the forearm bones at the wrist (see figure 3.5.4-5), you can prevent the sword arm from turning over and having complete range of motion. Keeping control of the wrist's direction and angle is crucial in maintaining connection with their sword.

**Hand over the thumb** – It is important to keep the hand pointing where you want the tip of the sword to point. You are controlling their *tiger's mouth* and awareness of your own wrist positioning will control their sword point *(see figure 3.5.6)*.

**Over the fingers** – When you grab and catch the opponent's hand over their grasp of the sword, you will have less control and difficulty maintaining the direction of their point. That being said, if you can bring their sword down to the earth and the tip down, this grip can keep their sword pinned (in any direction) as long as you are aware of the opponent's *tiger's mouth*.

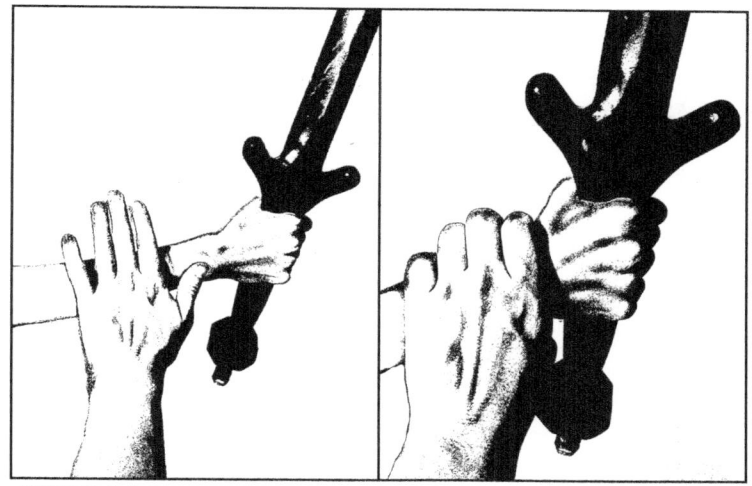

FIGURE 3.5.3
PRESSING THE FOREARM

FIGURE 3.5.4
GRASPING THE WRIST

FIGURE 3.5.5
GRASPING WRIST (ALT VIEW)

FIGURE 3.5.6
HOLDING THE HAND

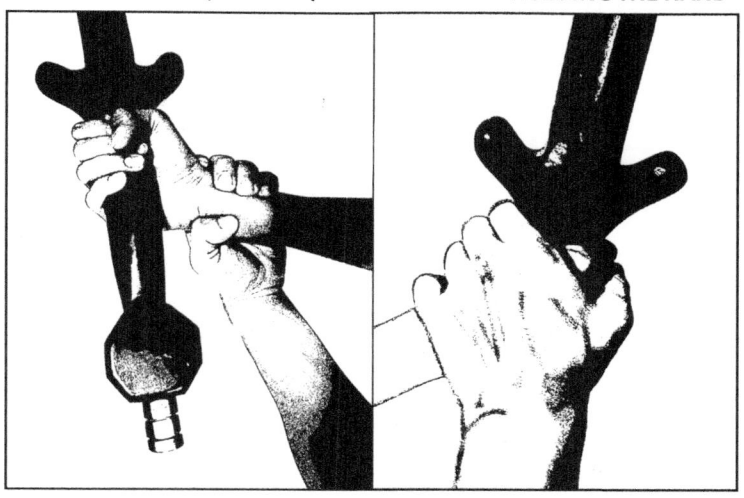

**Pommel** – The most superior of positions, grabbing the opponent's pommel, means you now have complete control over the rotation of the opponent's sword (see figure 3.5.7). As you take this grab, it is advised to retreat and withdraw your Swordsman's Hex to the rear position while pulling the pommel with you, and bringing your sword between you and the opponent.

This is the superior capture method to take the opponent's sword and ending the conflict without injury to either party.

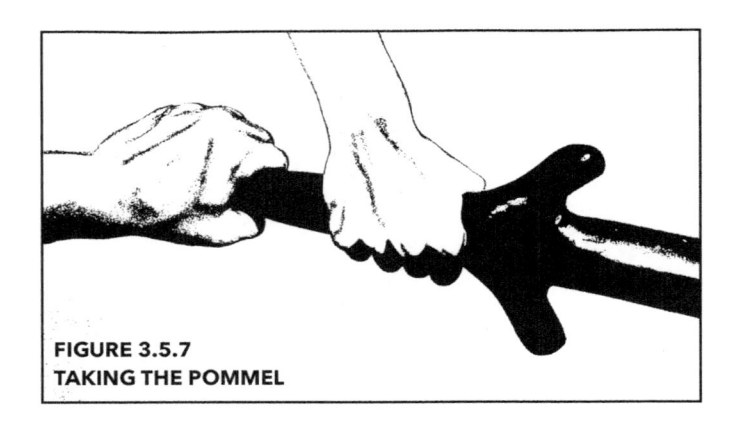

**FIGURE 3.5.7
TAKING THE POMMEL**

No matter which placement you have, it will be your weight, chest, shoulder, and elbow's combined strength which is now controlling the opponent's weapon. As they aim their sword with their wrist, you will aim their sword with your full left side of the body, and both hips.

The drills at the end of this chapter will help build these skills and prepare you for the the next chapter which will build on a few of the concepts presented here.

## Locking the Sword

A **Locked Sword** refers to when you control the opponent's pommel with your Swordsman's Hex hand and the point with your own sword. In this position, you control the direction of the opponent's sword, using their grab as the lever of the pivot. Meanwhile, your sword prevents the opponent from moving their hand towards you to offer a counter-cut.

Locking the sword is a great tactic for preparing to take the opponent's weapon. But it is important to be aware that your opponent may take this opportunity to implement wrestling or throwing techniques using their body weight and rushing in. You must not lay your weight on the opponent when they are locked, and realize when it is more opportune to release than to hold.

## DOUBLE-LOCKED SWORDS

Be wary of the **Double-Locked Swords**. In this scenario, both swordsman have grabbed each other's sword arms/

hand in some manner, and it becomes a battle of strength to control both/either sword. It is best to release a Locked Sword than to enter a Double-Locked Swords position.

When in this unfortunate scenario, the opponent will have many options in wrestling the swords or you. Stay attentive for their overwhelming force, as it may arise unexpectedly. As each angle and each grab will offer different forces and structures, it is important to be elusive and responsive. The swords are now to be considered wild animals thrashing in all directions.

Be gentle with your footwork. This is especially important when avoiding the blade, and the rushing of an opponent locked to both your arms. Much of Taijiquan appears in this scenario, but do not be pulled into holding ground and rooting deep unless you have the opponent at a loss and you are finalizing the throw or steal of the sword. One alignment change can put you down the line of either blade, and being aware of the initial principles are most important in this scenario.

# Fencing Drill 6 – Swordsman's Hex

Using the positions discussed in this chapter, the two swordsmen should apply the previous methods of controlling the central pillar, working the eight gates, and finding the correct position to utilize the Swordsman's Hex in a variety of ways.

Focusing on the pushing, grasping, grabbing, and stealing methods, the swordsmen should first avoid getting cut, and second avoid getting grabbed. The third concern is the double lock. All three of these situations should be avoided by both partners.

When double-locking often, this means the swordsmen are being too aggressive, and it should be fixed by the swordsmen lunging in to grab first by reducing his ferocity in the attack.

When the opponent single locks your sword often, this means you are not aligning your body and your wrist correctly. Going back to the first drills of foundation and alignment will help you maintain the sword in a more central position on your body, instead of holding out to the side or behind you.

Without this training, many will extend their pommel while blocking across their body. It is as if they are handing their sword to their opponent. Instead, find a way to move the body, and not only the sword.

When practicing this drill, if there is difficulty or confusion, it will be helpful to have one swordsman attempt to apply the swordsman's hex, while the other only tries to practice the previous principles. Once both swordsmen take a turn getting familiar with ways of attacking with the off-hand, both can resume working simultaneously to add the pressure of getting it correct quickly, and not waiting too much or over-baiting the opponent in a way that is not realistic in the briefness of a real sword exchange.

# Fencing Drill 7 – Double-locking

Although it is never recommended to enter a double-lock (even if you find this drill beneficial for your chances of survival), it is important to be familiar with what each type of movement does when in this scenario.

You and your fencing partner will cross swords with the handles to the right of the body. Both swordsmen place their off-hand the opponent's pommel/handle. With the swords crossed, and with the handles already grasped in one another's control, this drill begins from a double-locked position.

You will work three methods to become familiar with this position. The first will be to force and muscle each other. Feel the benefits and short coming of wrestling with one another while the swords are crossed. While using force, it is important to have excellent control over both swords by focusing on locking the opponent's weapon, and resisting their grab. You will notice that although one swordsman may be a stronger wrestler, it is blade awareness which can work to either swordsman's advantage. getting below your swords and pressing them upward will often give you the safest positioning, although the opponent's wrestling or kicking may come into play if you are defenseless with your footwork.

Once each swordsman is familiar with winning and losing this wrestling match, you will both switch to blade control. Instead of wrestling each other, you will wrestle the blades into one another's space. The goal will be to put the sword or swords in threatening positions to cause the opponent to disengage from the double lock. Be it bringing the blades across the opponent's arms or wrists, pressing them under their arms to get the blades close to the opponent's ribs and body, or having a lower position and getting one or both blades tangled with the opponent's legs.

This will all be done with strong wrist control on the sword arm, and good coordinated movement with the left elbow, shoulder, chest, and the hips. You will need to stay sensitive of when to give pressure and when to accept it for re-directive purposes in both sides of the body. Focusing on getting the most leverage on your sword-wielding wrist will counter the opponent's control on your sword. Your sword-wielding wrist will be important for controlling your opponent's blade. Your ability to resist their pommel-steering of your sword while you are directing the tip of their sword with your blade will help stabilize the combat in front of you.

Meanwhile, your swordsman's hex arm will help reduce how much control your opponent has over the engagement. Strong coordination with the left arm's joints will provide you with greater control over the opponent's weapon. Steering the opponent's weapon comes first, and your pressure with your blade is secondary. When not necessary, you may decide to disengage the swords to cut while controlling the opponent's weapon still.

The third method to be practiced is stepping and body movement. Jumping and squatting will break the opponent's ability to build a consistent plan of attack. Moving to your left will give you more control of the opponent's weapon, while moving to your right will give you more power for your sword arm. Moving in and out will allow you to break your opponent's rooted structure to reduce their ability to wrestle and use full body power.

Once trying all three of these practices, the swordsmen can bring them all together, and use these (and other methods) to cut or escape the double-lock.

# 6. Dividing The Army

When using the Swordsman's Hex to attack the opponent, you will be bringing their attention away from the sword (partially, if not entirely), and they will become concerned with the off-handed attack. Being aware of this in yourself should have been considered while practicing the previous methods in the fifth principle.

In "Dividing the Army," we are to utilize the lack of focus the opponent places on the sword to have an advantage in changes and manipulations on their blade. This idea of splitting the opponent's intention is similar to splitting their army into two lesser forces. As they go to match your advance on their position, you secretly will be applying the real pressure on the swords' positioning and alignment.

As the opponent becomes aware of this and fights to retain that position, your off-handed faint is now provided with the opportunity to become a legitimate attack or application of the Swordsman's Hex.

This is the practice of dividing the army, as one tries to gain leverage and advantages wherever the opponent is least defended.

Beyond the arms: positioning, change of levels, kicks, and even altering footwork can all offer different methods for breaking the concentration the opponent has in making the correct responsive action with their sword. It is important to capitalize on either opportunity, and do not take risks or offer openings.

## Avoid Gambling

It is not encouraged or recommended to offer limbs or opportunities to the opponent in exchange for openings– when discussing dividing the opponent's intention. If they do not feel a true threat which requires an adjustment in their current actions to be thwarted, then you are only dividing yourself. Gambling with your life or your limbs only encourages them to stick to their original attack, as they are no longer threatened by inadequate taunts and faints.

By dividing the opponent's army, you are also dividing your own to some degree. Because your focus is on the balance between the two opportunities, you are only more aware if your opponent is fooled or threatened. If they are not aware of the secondary attack, or do not concern themselves with it, you are only weakening your own focus.

Because of these issues, it's important to only divide the opponent's army when you yourself have the leverage and advantages. Even if they are hidden in the moment, the opponent may not perceive the situation the way you do.

## Preventing a Divided Army

No matter how you react to their simultaneous attacks from both sides, you must make sure your action is qualified and of threat to their current course of action. It is important to bring their intention to your attack, as to re-establish a single front.

When the opponent has the Central Pillar, and you are in the engagement range for their *hex hand*, then you are at the greatest disadvantage and most susceptible to being divided. You must be steadfast with your cuts, and keep to movements which either attack their sword hand, or bring the swords to where they must cross the line of combat to reach you.

When the opposing swordsman reaches in, you responding with constant pressure on their blade, while withdrawing slightly, can now have your blade in range for their grasp instead of your hand or pommel. This will make the pressure more intense on your own sword, as you are now defending closer to the leaf (tip of the sword). Be considerate of the adjustment as their response may be sudden and severe.

Turning the wrist clockwise, while stepping clockwise, and moving from the Fire to the Lake gates, you can enter with your sword hand and bring the Central Pillar to the point of their off-hand's attack or line of pursuit. This is also practical in the reverse when moving from the Mountain to Water trigrams.

Extending your position forward to enter with your Swordsman's Hex, you may be offered an opportunity to divide the opponent simultaneously with their counter attack. But it is most important to not allow the swords to be double-locked with the enemy's, or begin a chase of circling through the gates haphazardly.

# Fencing Drill 8 – Dividing the Army

Building off the previous drills, instead of focusing on using the swordsman's hex hand to gain the advantage, you will focus on using it to change the opponent's shape and attacking with your sword. The goal here is to cut the opponent more so than to take their sword. But it is important both parts of the attack are done with honesty of intent.

When offensively applying this skill, the swordsman will take the central pillar, lead in an attack with the swordsman's hex to cause the opponent to adjust their sword-wielding arm/hand position. Taking advantage of this movement, the swordsman will continue their blade's attack. At this point, the defender may decide which attack takes priority, and the swordsman attacking will respond with their full intention to the least defended attack.

When applied defensively, as the opposing swordsman reaches in with the swordsman's hex, bringing the central pillar back towards that line of combat will help to bring their intention back into their blade, and negate their reach with the left hand. If they do not reconsider their extension, the blades should be brought to a position that can endanger or cut the over-extended left hand.

As you convince them to defend, use your swordsman's hex to attack, once again dividing their army. When performed correctly, you should now have superior position. Be mindful of over aggressive partners, and be ready to move backwards when they are attempting to get the cut from a central position.

# 7. Controlling Initiative

When two swords are engaged, the swordsman who is controlling the action and dictating the changes would be said to have **initiative**.

In an active engagement where both swordsmen are vying for positioning and opportunity only one swordsman's intended action can happen in the moment. Applying the principles of Yin-Yang Theory, it could be said that the sword that has the yang (or creative) force, has initiative.

In the engagement, the swordsman with initiative is also the swordsman that is under the least threat in the moment. By being the one without initiative, you are constantly responding to the threat (or potential threat) the other swordsman is placing you in. By having initiative, this means your actions are working and therefore the swords are where you will them to be.

Although it is not necessarily advised to always *have* initiative, it is encouraged to always do your best to *control* initiative. Deciding each moment to give up initiative, instead of losing it in the exchanges, gives the swordsman many opportunities to retake initiative and set the opponent up into more opportune positions and application scenarios.

## TAIJI THEORY FOR INITIATIVE

When applying Taiji Theory to swordplay, the terms Yin and Yang will need to be defined in a way that can be discussed in context. For the purpose of discussing initiative, the term Yang will be used for the sword that is being creative, while the term Yin will refer to the sword that is being receptive.

The idea of Taiji Theory for discussing initiative can help by breaking down every action into **beats**. A beat refers to every moment in which a change can occur. In any given beat, the yang sword will be moving the engagement in the way the swordsman wills and visualizes. In that same beat, the yin sword is being manipulated, and must respond accordingly.

We can see the Taiji as the total balance of these Yin and Yang forces. When being Yin, one is responding to the will of the opponent. In the Yin moments, one may be under threat and defending, one may be returning to natural from an overextend position, or possibly the swordsman is studying the opponent and getting a feel for their timing, shapes, and habits.

But yin and yang in Taiji are not isolated or absolute. They are blending constantly, filling the gaps in each other's space. A truly balanced sword fight will have both swords constantly manifesting half of each swordsman's will seemingly simultaneously. As each swordsman adjusts to cut off one another's beats, they may change the Yin-Yang balance so minutely in different ways that it creates a sense of constant "no threat; always threat."

It is important to find your own internal balance of being receptive and responsive while being creative and resistant.

As levels of force build and release, it can be compared to the total taiji getting larger or smaller. When the two forces meet equally and nothing happens, they are equal parts yin and yang each. As one begins to manipulate the other, the one sword takes the yang presence. As the swordsman responds, they may or may not take back the initiative (or become the majority-yang sword), but they may reduce the threat, and add a level of redirection or creative movement. This is the sword regaining some Yang presence through creative actions.

## HARMONY AND DISHARMONY

A **beat**, as described previously, refers to any given moment in which a change can occur. As two swordsmen take action, they may work on the same beats, or work to go off timing from each other. Both tactics have their benefits, but both rely on a feeling of the opponent's rhythm. Hearing this rhythm can only be found by yin moments and a sense of listening to the opponent's way of changing and responding.

When the swordsmen stay on beat with one another, often time this builds a sense of momentum between them. Allowing cuts to change back and forth, the force and power may build up, until there is a break in the swords or a break in timing. This is considered **harmonious swordplay**. The attitude is straight forward and orthodox, and it can be very comfortable in the moment (for better or worse).

When one swordsman breaks the rhythm, and attacks between beats, off-beat, or quits the engagement, they are considered to be using **disharmonious swordplay**. This is used to take action when one feels they will out act the opponent's reaction, or cause a break in the flow. Movements that cause "knee-jerk reactions" and sudden breaks are considered disharmonious.

It is important not to bring judgement into swordplay with these terms. Harmony and disharmony are both found in nature, and both exist at different times, as yin and yang to one another. It is important to be prepared in every given moment for the opponent to act harmoniously or disharmoniously.

In the harmonious moments, the momentum and movement take turns as the swordsmen exchange initiative back and forth like chess. As they pick up speed and pressure, it is forcing the players to make decisions with less time and consideration, but they are still moving in response to one another in some sense of balance.

In the disharmonious moments, the swordsmen battle for initiative by changing in ways that disrupt the other swordsman's momentum, causing a reactive action with a less-well-thought-out posture. By moving on beats in which the opponent is carrying momentum, you now are making a creative action in which the opponent must change their momentum to respond to.

## Four Phases of Momentum

When two swords are engaged with equal pressure, there is no room for momentum to build. When one sword suddenly moves out of the way or reduces their resistance rapidly, the pushing sword may build momentum. This momentum will cause the sword to move suddenly and often times have a greater sized swing or thrust than the original intent.

Another example for generating momentum is when a swordsman sees an opportunity to cut, and rapidly attacks in the moment, hoping to change faster than the opponent can respond.

In both of these examples, when the swordsman has momentum, they have spaced out their beats across more moments. This means they can not change as often or quickly, until the momentum is spent. The more momentum one has, the bigger the movements, the slower the reaction, due to an increased amount of power required to change one's own force.

But the sword with momentum also has the benefit of additional power. The sword carrying more momentum will overpower another, as the weight of the sword and the strength of the swordsman are considered part of how much momentum one generates. Attacking with momentum can cause the opponent to react harshly to one's increased force, and that stiffness or frailty can lead to successful cuts.

A sword carrying momentum also carries speed. Any fast movement requires momentum as it builds upon the previous moments to project forward in to the next. As a sword begins to move, it is committing to speeding up, being fast, and slowing down, before returning to stationary and changing directions. There is a unique relationship between speeding up and slowing down, which is affected by many attributes. These include, but are not limited to: weight of the sword, resistance given by the opponent, strength of the swordsman, amount of momentum being generated, correct structures and generation of power. The general principle would be that the more you build up, the more beats, effort, and intention it will take to slow down.

Depending on the technique and one's skill, different tools can be used to find benefits in each of these phases. But changes will be more difficult to control when acting at faster speeds. In addition to the momentum broadening the movements, the more speed one develops, the less control one has. As the velocity of the sword increases, each action has fewer beats to act upon in the same amount of time.

Being able to apply the correct force, at the correct time, to cause the correct change, in the correct moment, while keeping the technique in the correct place and on the correct path, requires a deep understanding of both your own skill and your opponent's. Adding momentum may give more beats to your opponent than you can react to. To do a technique slow and smooth in practice, the movement is precise and tight. But when the movement is given speed and power (and therefore momentum), it now will require more active force to respond correctly. The correct amount of momentum to work with should be discovered by knowing how much is too much for you to react effectively in defense.

## RELINQUISHING INITIATIVE

When you are deciding to be yin and receptive of the opponent, you may be partially receptive, and partially resistant. You may limit the swords from coming towards your face, but allow them to go away or downward. These types of controlled resistances are one way of controlling the opponent's options while relinquishing initiative to them in the next beat.

Being actively aware of all directions in which the engagement can change, and being able to open or close gate changes made available to your opponent is important in a long game strategy and in creating your own openings. By giving your opponent options to change into and limiting others, it is hoped the opponent will choose the seemingly best option, although all the changes are designed around your own techniques and postures.

When you relinquish initiative, it is important not to understand this as giving in entirely. It can be considered relinquishing the role as the major yang force in the movement of the swords for that beat. It is not a total submission of staying yin and being defeated instantly. Use the balance of yin and yang to keep yourself aligned and structured, while providing options that seem promising for the opponent to take advantage of.

# Fencing Drill 9 – Harmonious Swordplay

To understand initiative, first the swordsman should become familiar with harmonious swordplay. The two swordsmen will make an agreement to not surprise or startle each other with explosive or unexpected techniques. The two will engage swords and fence naturally, trying to find the best positioning to take initiative and be the one cutting. As you parry each other's cuts, it will be similar to taking turns, although not consistent in how many cuts each may take. The swordsmen will feel how to guide the opponent's weapon to better places for their own cuts, and see how initiative naturally changes hands and how one maintains it by preventing the opponent's strategies to regain constant control.

Going with one another, this will be like the game of chess or weiqi. The swordsmen will work to break the opponent's positions and structures until the swords are in the opponent's spaces and there is an opening for cutting. Cutting is not a point in this drill, nor is it a game. There may be no successful cuts here if both swordsmen are practicing slowly and understand the previous principles presented in this book.

It is encouraged to slow down just before landing cuts as a way to realign your beats with your partners for this exercise.

# Fencing Drill 10 – Disharmonious Swordplay

This drill will begin with the partners practicing harmonious swordplay, but one will be designated the chaotic element which will break from the harmony to take cuts that are not with the rhythm of combat established. The partner should respond correctly and protect themselves. The goal will be to take startling opportunities as the chaotic element swordsman breaks harmony to gain initiative. The defending swordsman will focus on reacting to startling and disharmonious elements as well.

After both swordsmen get a chance to try this method, they will then act simultaneous to fence in a very unpredictable manner. The engagements may break when taking cuts, so it will be important not to let the strategy or excitement leave opportunities for dirty cuts.

One of the biggest short comings of using disharmonious techniques will be the opportunities for dirty cuts. Because the essence of disharmonious swordplay is moving in a way which the opponent cannot respond to quickly enough, this means their response may be going for an attack before they realize they are under threat as well. If you find yourselves cutting one another seemingly simultaneously, then your strategies for gaining initiative are flawed and the swordsmen are not looking far enough in advance. You must always consider where your sword is, and where your opponent's is going.

# 8. Holding the Lines

In Taiji Theory, we hold two foundational elements of force; linear and circular. When one is shifting towards, away, or across their opponent, they are applying in linear force. When one rotates their hips and waist, they add a circular force. Taiji's strength is often found in the delicately crafted balance between these two types of power.

These two types of power are both very applicable and appropriate when discussing the sword's engagement. When applying linear power, it is often used to press on the opponent's blade, and lock them into place or take ground and position. When applying a circular force, you are generally deflecting, escaping, and rerouting the opponent's lines of force to find a better path for your pressure to enter the space. Because of this, we label these two types of force Yang and Yin Pressures.

When "holding the lines," one is using their positioning, structure, and alignment to the opponent to prevent their advantages, instead of moving the sword. Often times this includes stepping, rotating, and shifting while responding the the opponent. With the correct type of response with appropriate footwork, the sword changes can be negated, and new opportunities can be presented as the opponent is forced into an unfamiliar space.

If the opponent works to push your sword to the left, you will have the choice to resist the push or let it move. In both circumstances, the most novice fencers will hold their ground and allow the sword to move from the arm and shoulder. As one advances in the art, this movement will move down to the waist and hips.

But a primary skill necessary in the speed of combat is for the movement of the sword to also move from the feet. If the opponent chooses to push the swordsman's blade left, being able to side step left with the pressure instead of having the arm move, keeps your structure, and prevents a break in alignment. This loose stepping and fast rising-falling skill will hold the body's structure and alignment, to keep the force and power consistently available.

Allowing the opponent to push your sword alone is not always an issue, but one must be competent enough to know when the movement comes from the wrist, elbow, shoulder, waist, hips, knees, or ankles for the most promising positioning and opportunities.

## Extending though the Sword

When pushed on by an external force, the swordsman has three basic options. They may resist by pushing down the line of force against the opponent; they may go with the force by following and guiding that line with it's original intention, or they may send that force in an assisted and alternate direction.

Similar to getting behind the cart to help push, there are many ways to get behind a force and add power. One of these is found in extending.

If an opponent strikes directly towards you, by pushing against that force perpendicularly, you can redirect that power as it comes with you. Similarly, if a force is pushing across your extension, the force will combine with yours and be redirected to some degree.

This technique of extending through the tip of the sword is the method used to add the opponent's force to your own, instead of resisting their power.

The technique is performed by using the eyes and visualizing the reach of the sword (sometimes visualized as qi or energy extending out the tip), in the direction it points to hold the position or movement. As the counter/parry/blocking force is applied across your positioning, the use of the eyes and intention to extend out the tip of the sword will apply this redirection of force by aligning the body appropriately to hold the structure, instead of breaking the structure to use the muscles and body to resist the opponent's suggested changes.

Relaxing into this reach will help give your body a fast reaction and ability to change. Having a firm or solid reach will leave you susceptible to your opponents changes in rhythm and intention.

## The Swordsman's Hex

As briefly discussed earlier, an additional benefit to the swordsman's hex is it's activation of the left side of the body. By applying this same reaching or extending feeling out from the fingers of the hex hand, the left side of the body is now also activated to hold the structure of the sword. With the two sides of the body supporting one another, the opponent's use of pushing and pressing against your sword will lose a great amount of leverage.

Extending the sword finger at the proper angles is important as we do not want to hold a straight line between the sword and the sword finger. By over extending the chest and pinching the shoulder blades together, you will lose a great amount of structure and force.

Instead, use the natural curve of the body as allow your line of intention to have a curve as it moves through your body. It will be rare to have the chest open more than 135 degrees (except perhaps when thrusting).

Once the body is reinforced, by the left hand, it is important not to allow this to stiffen your movements. By changing the swordsman's hex earlier than the sword, you can anchor your new line for the next position. By studying your forms, you will find many examples of the left hand moving to prepare for the next position and have a consistency of force and stability in the changes.

## Cutting the Opponent's Changes

When the opponent goes to circle around the Central Pillar, the movement of your position can negate these changes. By holding the line with the body, and using the feet to adjust your positioning to the opponent's sword (instead of the opponent themselves), you can hold one position without combating the opponent.

An example of this would be if the opponent circles around to your left side, you may move back at a 45 degree diagonal to keep the swords in the same place in relationship to your body and position.

Another example would be if you wish to push the opponent's sword to your right while in an outward engagement. Often times, a fencer will open their chest and elbow and press from the body. Holding the line could be done in at least three ways for this action:

 Rotating from the heavenly pillar of the body to press across while extending the line will move the swords over without changing the relationship of the shoulder to the sword. In this method, you are turning the hips and/or waist to move the central pillar.

2. Side stepping to the right while holding the line through the body will move the opponent's sword with you. In this way, you are using your leg and hip strength to move the central pillar. One must remember that the opponent may be encouraged to step as a response to your step.

3. Opening the line from a narrow shape (sword finger in a *more forward* position), to a more open and obtuse angle through

the body. This is done by the expansion of the thorax and the opening of the shoulders, as one extends out both the sword and swordsman's hex.

## Aligning for Cuts

In the circumstances of cutting and swinging, it is important to consider when one should have the most control available to them. In cutting, there are fast loose cuts, and solid reinforced cuts. Depending on which type of cut you are throwing, your use of the lines will vary.

When throwing a fast loose cut, it is important to put the sword finger and intention in the place where you will need to be ready to change. when your cut gets to it's place of change, you should be able to use all nine palaces of the body in unison to make the quickest and most controlled change possible. If you cut through your solid structural range, you will have less power to do the change, and therefore it will happen slower and with less available force to deal with the opponent's continued will pressing on you.

When utilizing a strong reinforced cut, it is important to use the line as the guide that is constantly pulling you to the next moment. By allowing the line of intention and force to move gradually in front of your cut, you are practicing a type of *leading skill* which gives your body the sensation of being pulled, like water being irrigated.

## THREATENING LINES

As covered in the initial fencing exercises, when the tip of the sword is pointed at the opponent directly, their instinct should be to parry or move the sword away. Using your line to threaten the opponent can be an excellent tool to build pressure, energy, and nervousness in the opponent.

As the opponent works to parry your sword, deciding to reinforce it with the line of intention or to stir the wrist quickly to get to the other side of their blade are two examples of utilizing the line. As they assume the force of the line is there, you may choose to release it or hold it. When the opponent's force is strong, you can respond by getting out of their line. When the opponent is light and soft, you can apply your lines to give pressure without additional tensions in your movements and structure.

A threatening line is an excellent tool to force the opponent's movements. As you give them threatening structure instead of momentum, there arrises a tension in the opponent if they do not respond using their own lines and correct movement.

# Fencing Drill 11 – Holding the Lines

This practice method is used to increase the quality of each swordsman's footwork and spacial awareness in regards to their opponent. Like many of the previous drills, each swordsman will attempt the drill with their partner, before switching roles, and then trying it simultaneously.

Once the swords are engaged, the first to try this method will respond to the opponent's offensive movements with footwork, and minimal sword changes. Instead of pushing the sword left and right, up and down, the swordsman will use their wrist for angling the sword, use their sword finger for holding structure, and use their steps and sinks to react and attack. Using the legs and body to move the sword, the swordsman should begin to understand good and bad stepping concepts in terms of confronting the opponent's free moving weapon. By staying engaged and maintaining initiative, this method works best when the opponent is pursuing with strength and force. The partner should not use aggressive disharmony until this skill has been developed with harmonious changes first.

Once ready, add this practice into your free fencing using all the previous fencing principles as well.

# 9. Three Types of Cohesion

**Cohesion** is the term used to describe when two swordsmen are both participating in keeping the swords in interaction. This means that both swordsmen are responding to one another, while working to simultaneously take advantage of any opportunities presented to end the conflict. Cohesion can come in three forms. Just as Daoism describes, the human is made of the **three treasures**: **jing**, **qi**, and **shen**. These three types of cohesion correspond directly to these three treasures. The Chinese terms can be roughly translated as corporeal, energetic, and cerebral (respectively). All aspects of the human experience and manifestations can be linked to one of these three categories.

Jing, or the corporeal body, refers to all the physical parts of the human. The organs, muscles, tissues, bones, blood, fluids, and facia, are all aspects of one's jing. The materials we are made up of and the things you would find in an autopsy all are included.

In terms of cohesion in fencing, corporeal cohesion refers to anytime the swords are touching and the swordsmen can sense one another's pressure and changes. This physical connection is what is discussed in this book throughout most of the previous chapters.

When discussing Qi–or the energy of the human–we are discussing any type of change, combustion, or use of stored energy in the system, taking action. When you use your muscles, oxygen is used, turning blood blue, and giving the body the ability to change shapes and overcome external forces. When one digests what has been eaten, the nutrients are changed into productive new cells in the body. This change is also an example of qi. As one puts effort into their strike, they are exerting more of their own qi, or effort, or force. There may or may not be mystical components to the discussion of qi, depending on the person speaking. But the life of the body requires the ability to produce changes; both chemical and structural. Therefore, these are all classified as one's qi, or one's energetic component.

As we discuss fencing, an energetic cohesion refers to when the swords are chasing one another through rhythm and pattern, instead of physically touching. As two swords lose a physical connection, if they maintain a similar pattern, the energy of each sword will keep them chasing one another. So, in the case of the swords coming apart, the energetic cohesion is when the swords are physically chasing one another, although they may or may not have a physical connection.

The term shen is often described as the spiritual component to the human being. This should include all mental activity: conscious and subconscious. One's shen includes all the mental processes in one's mind. If one were to imagine lifting their arm into the air, the image created in the mind is in the realm of the mind-scape, and is not a physical manifestation. But shen is also the director or the general of the jing, sending the orders through the qi as the messaging system. If one imagines lifting their arm in a particular fashion, then they actively move their arm to match that image, this is shen directing qi to manifest change in the jing.

In terms of fencing, any type of strategy or interplay of planning and foresight can be a form of mental cohesion. If the opponent draws back, and the swordsman enters in and threatens with the tip, this is a cohesion of shen, as one sees the spaces being opened and closed.

Leading the opponent in to these positions is another manifestation of this spiritual cohesion.

As one works through the previous eight principles presented in this book, they will mostly be working on a state of cohesion of jing, or a physical cohesion. As the next nine principles are introduced in the following volume, they will discuss the connection and the initiation of cohesion with an opponent that may intend on chopping or swinging the sword instead of a taiji fencing strategy. In the meantime, it will be important to see how you and various opponents lead and follow in the exchange, while experiencing all three of these cohesions.

By starting with a physical engagement, the swordsmen can feel the pressure change and adjust, leading the swords to better or worse alignments. As the two swordsmen gain a familiarity with this physical cohesion, they will begin to find each others' rhythms and reactive responses when disharmony appears. Once the two swordsmen can gauge one another, the swords may drift apart while still feeling the other's flow. When the swords are no longer physically touching, the swordsman will have three options: to reconnect, to take a cut, or to predict the other's movements. These moments where the swords are responding to the motions and changes of one another while no longer physically touching will be your opportunity to study the energetic cohesion.

Once the swords break apart, and the two swordsmen realize that mutual destruction is a bad plan, the swords will both be responding to each other's body alignments, stepping, rhythm changes, and momentums, with and without physical engagement. As the two swordsmen compete to see who's strategy will be applied, they will be constantly preventing one another from moving into superior position. Both swordsmen will now be working in a level of mental or spiritual cohesion.

The process must be built like this, from jing to qi to shen. If you attempt to reverse the order, and begin by reacting to the opponent's attacks from a disengaged position, you will be training the eye to respond perhaps, but you will not be training the cohesion of shen. Being able to cut off their attack because you have become familiar with their methods does not help you when you are in the engagement, as much as when you are entering the engagement. As opponent's change, these reductive habits will give you false responses, instead of sensitive and tuned ones.

None of these types of cohesion are limited only to themselves. In most cases, swordsmen are applying all three types of cohesion, but the more tangible, the more dominant it's signals will be. Therefore, physical cohesion will be more noticeable than energetic cohesion. While energetic will be more thought-consuming than spiritual cohesion.

# Fencing Drill 12 – Matching the Corporeal

Corporeal Cohesion has actually been the focus during most of these exercises. Here though, the two swordsmen will engage one another's blade, and work to maintain cohesion, even when cutting. Each swordsmen will first take turns attempting to make cuts without disengaging. At first, this may feel like harmonious swordplay, but the harmony can be in all forms of cohesion.

Once each swordsman has become familiar with doing this practice, it is encouraged to attempt these skills while both swordsmen's feet are fixed. Much like fixed-step pushing hands, this method will keep both swordsmen in range of one another, and work on developing the physical sensitivity.

Once each swordsman has had an opportunity to try, then they both may work against one another simultaneously. It is important to remember this is about making a cut while maintaining a physical connection between the blades. Swordsmen should not be disengaging in attempt to take cuts. This drill is saved for the later stages of initial fencing skill development as a way to return to the idea of cohesion, and step back from any developed obsession or one-mindedness towards taking cuts.

# Fencing Drill 13 – Matching the Energetic

After you have established the physical cohesion, the swordsmen can use this as a base point to explore energetic cohesion. It is important to remember that energetic cohesion does not require the swordsmen start with physical cohesion, but it is encouraged to do so when learning the practices.

Starting with a stirring energy, the two swordsmen will engage blades and begin parrying the opponent's blade in a circular motion. This should be practiced both clockwise and counter-clockwise. As the swords push one another, the swordsman that feels like they are being chased should attempt to disengage and continue the flow of the circle. This may cause the opponent to follow the blade, even though no clear threat is established.

This feeling of still following the momentum of the swords and the movement's of the opponent's weapon without the continued physical cohesion will begin developing a sense of the swords. This will be a combination of habit, visual cues, physical sensitivity, and spiritual one-mindedness. Being in the moment, the swords push and pull each other with their empty space, more so than applying force direction onto the other's blade.

As one swordsman starts to lead, the other will practice following. It is important as the leader to keep yourself defended, and keep your motions in directions and patterns that would be in line with your opponent's goals, and not frivolous or at random. Keeping your opponent's energy engaged and chasing your advances is the key to keeping them from cutting at you when the blades are not touching one another.

After both swordsmen attempt to lead and follow, both may begin moving in and out of physical cohesion. Losing contact to maintain the sense of a single engagement through energetic cohesion will allow the swordsman to better manage timing, momentum, and pressure changes.

Once this exercise can be practiced from the stir, is it also good to try this with horizontal cutting strikes, figure-eight cuts, and then with free movement. If at any point you feel like you are strategizing more than pushing and pulling the swords, then you will be ready to move onto the third cohesion practice methods.

# Fencing Drill 14 – Matching the Strategic

Now that you are capable at maintaining physical cohesion and interacting with energetic cohesion, it will be time now to study your mental cohesion. In this practice, the swordsmen should pay attention to three key components: one's own strategy, the opponent's changes and patterns, and the level of mutual awareness the opponent has developed.

As swordsmen progress in their skill, they become more and more aware of when to take a cut and when not to. Often times, an opening for a cut is visible, but the reaction of the opponent may be hidden by the intensity of the moment. A novice martial artist will make attempts for cuts that put themselves at risk to have the cut returned or countered. Meanwhile, a well seasoned swordsman will hold off from attacking any openings which do not have safe escapes planned in advance.

In this drill, the two swordsmen will face off with swords threatening one another, but without cohesion. As each swordsman moves around to avoid the opponent's cuts, the swordsmen should use their sword to parry and offer counter cuts. These cuts should only be taken when the opponent cannot return the attack. One should work to out maneuver the opponent via threatening them with the potential of the next cut, and not risk taking a cut if it means the opponent's response will go unanswered.

Each swordsman should avoid physical cohesion and contact entirely unless parrying, and will find energetic cohesion throughout the exchange. When being parried, it is important to avoid contact as the attacker, and give them a new strategy to work against. As the two swords dance around one another, each swordsman will begin to find awareness of their own movements and which ways the opponent reacts to their sword.

Just as the other types of cohesion, there are many training methods to explore this principle. Starting from this mutual threat and looking to convince the opponent to defend instead of holding an attack position will be the first steps to manipulating the opponent's strategy through your own movements and changes.

# Fencing Drill 15 – Balancing the Principles

Now that all the foundational taiji fencing principles have been covered, it is important to practice these skills with a variety of partners and opponents. Bringing all of these skills together against one person is excellent for learning to defeat a particular foe. But it is only through a wide array of styles and methods can one improve their own skill overall.

The final drill presented will be to practice all of the previous methods combined, considering when each one has a moment of opportunity, and when the particular tools will lead you into traps and pitfalls. When engaged, it is important to ask yourself what would the potential outcomes be in a particular engagement depending on which principle–or principles–you apply. By examining how you might use them, you will begin to improve your reactionary time, and improve your correct response rate.

Keep in mind that open fencing should be practiced with honest and mutual support. Letting your partner know when you have received a cut and avoiding the dreaded mutual cut will help to refine the skills of all who participate.

When open fencing, remember to take many breaks. Do not fence with a tired wrist or sore arm. Keep attacks to the head/face close, but avoid any cuts which you do not have the control to stop. If you find yourself swinging with momentum, or hearing the swords bang together, it should be assumed you are moving too recklessly, and without enough control. Avoid this momentum and keep the practice clean. A dirty or ugly fight leads to both swordsmen's demise.

# Glossary

Alignment – An understanding of the proper order of things. Correct alignment leads to improved structure and function.

Attack – The action of trying to harm or make contact with the opponent.

Attacker – The person with the intent of causing harm to the opponent.

Avoid – The action of responding to an attack by being out of the line of the cut.

Bagua – The umbrella term for all arts related to Baguazhang. The term comes from the image of the eight trigrams.

Baguajian – The sword art that is practiced after foundational training in Baguazhang.

Baguatu – The image of the taijitu surrounded by the eight trigrams.

Baguazhang – An empty-hand martial practice focused on applying the Yijing and Baguatu principles to self-defense and/or combat.

Balance (principle) – The use of the left hand to stabilize the body and–in turn–the sword.

Balance (personal) – Your state of equilibrium which provides structure and alignment.

Balance (sword) – A factor in determining the quality of a sword. Traditional Taiji fencing is best practiced with a sword balanced as close to the guard as possible.

Beat – The shortest measurement of time in the moment; The pace determined by the cuts of the swords and momentum produced.

Blade – The cutting and engaging portion of the sword. Everything above the hilt.

Brace – To use structure to receive force.

Capture – To take (or take control of) the opponent's weapon.

Cast – The act of performing spells and magical practices in traditional Daoist religion, often times done with the swordsman's hex when a sword is not readily available.

Central Pillar – The point of engagement.

Circle of Engagement – the area in which a swordsman can reach while rotating around the Point of Engagement

Corporeal – Any aspect of the physical person. The bones, blood, flesh, muscles, skin, etc.

Cut (action) – To use intention and action to attempt to injure or touch the opponent with the edge of one's sword.

Cut (state) – After one is touched by the opponent's blade.

Dantian – The center of equilibrium of the body, found in the lower abdomen, between the hip bones.

Dao – Chinese term for the guiding principle(s) of the universe and it's manifestation. This term is often translated as "The Way" or the natural path of the universe.

Dao – Chinese term for a saber or large cutting knife.

Daoism – The traditional religion of China dedicated to finding harmony with the Dao and it's cosmology.

Daoist Swordsman – A swordsman that relates their sword practice to the study and worship of formal Daoist religion.

Daoist Swordsmanship – The art which is cultivated and practiced through training sword with Daoist philosophies and theory applied.

Defend – The action of responding to the opponent's cuts and intention

Disharmonious Swordplay – When a swordsman breaks rhythm to startle the opponent in an unpredictable way.

Diving the Army – When one makes the opponent defend in multiple locations simultaneously.

Double-Lock – When both swordsmen have the opponent's sword locked.

Drills – The act of practicing a single technique or concept with repetition.

Edge – The sharpened portion of the blade.

Eight Gates – The eight positions around the body where the swords can be engaged. Pointing up or down, chest is open or closed, sword is pushing inward or outward.

Eight Trigrams – All possible combinations when combining yin and yang with three factors in two forms. Made up of 3 solid or split lines, trigrams represent various combinations of creativity and receptivity.

Energy – Any force used to cause changes to the physical realm. Breath, digestion, and effort all use and manipulate one's energy.

Engage – To meet the opponent's blade and work to keep the connection.

Engagement – When the two swords are crossed.

Evade – To move out of the way of a particular cut or action.

Fencing – The sport of sword-fighting.

Five Defenses – The five general responses available when dealing with an attacking opponent.

Form – A position or shape that has its own inherent values when studied. A static posture is an example of a form. One may use any stance and static posture to define a form.

Formset – A choreographed sword dance passed on from generation to generation. These often hold the keys to a particular style or methodology when practiced for extended periods.

Gongfu – Any skill that requires practice to be good at or find proficiency in.

Grab – To hold the opponent in some manner in your off-hand.

Grapple – To fight with the opponent in a wrestling or clinch fighting fashion.

Guard (posture) – The position one holds when awaiting the opponent's attack, or preparing one's own.

Guard (section of sword) – The portion of the sword between the handle and the blade, often used to protect the hand from the blades.

Handle – The portion of the sword designed to be held with one or two hands.

Harmonious Swordplay – When two swordsmen respect one another's pace and rhythm during combat.

Heavenly Pillar – The figurative description of the spine like post that rises through a person's body.

Hilt – All parts of the sword below the blade. This includes the pommel, handle, and guard.

Holding the Line – The action of using total structure power as a whole when responding, instead of only moving the sword in various directions.

Initiative – The state of being yang in combat, and leading the opponent to respond.

Inward Engagement – When the sword are crossed and both swordsmen are pushing inward, as if trying to close the chest.

Inward Position – Same as an inward engagement.

Hold – When one grabs in a way to keep the thing stationary in space.

Jian – Chinese term for the straight sword used in taiji fencing.

Jing – A reference term for all of the physical components to the human body. Our blood, bones, and nerves are all examples of parts of the human's jing.

Knife – A short dagger or blade held in the off-hand, and often times hidden.

Kung Fu – An old translation of the term gongfu.

Laozi – The attributed founder of the first Daoist scripture, the Daodejing.

Lead – To have the opponent follow one's actions.

Line of Combat – The straight line between the two swordsman's central pillars.

Line of Engagement – The line between the two swordsman, tracing down their arm and meeting at the point of engagement. This is different from the line of combat, as it curves through the structures of the engaged swordsmen.

Locked – When a swordsman has control of the engagement with their sword, and the opponent's arm/pommel with the off-hand.

Meditation – Any practice that requires stillness in in the body, or a constant state of focus.

Mixed Engagement – When a left-handed swordsman and a right-handed swordsmen cross blades to engage. An inward or outward engagement may be considered mixed, and will be defined by the right-handed swordsman's position.

Movement – A single change from one stance to another with corresponding hands and body changes. A movement can be seen as a single action of changing. Stringing movements together, one creates a posture.

Mujian – Chinese term for wooden swords.

Off-hand – The hand which does not hold the primary sword.

Off-handed Weapon – Any item used in the left hand as secondary tool.

Opponent – Those in which you are trying to make cuts on, or avoiding cuts from. The opposing swordsman in an engagement.

Outward Engagement – When the swords are crossed and both swordsmen are pressing outward on each other's blades.

Outward Position – Another term for an outward engagement.

Partner – The person with whom you are fencing with in an educational or training environment.

Point of Engagement – The point in space where the two swords meet one another.

Pommel – The weighted ended of the sword used to counter-balance the blade and for striking when the blade is unavailable.

Posture – A single idea being expressed in a stance or movement. Some postures are a single movement in a single stance, a single movement between two stances, or a single idea through a compilation of stances and movements.

Prepare – To position the body or Swordsman's Hex in a way that enhances the following techniques, and not simply to perform the current action.

Press – When one uses their body weight and shifting to manipulate the engagement.

Push – When one uses the extension of their arms and changes in their structure to manipulate the engagement.

Push Hands – A common english translation for the taiji practice of tuishou. This practice is used to develop sensitivity, timing, alignment, and application for health and combat.

Push Swords – A common english translation of tuijian, the practice of pushing the swords to develop sensitivity in the engagement. Push swords and taiji fencing are at times interchangeable, although push swords generally does not include disengaging to cut or pierce.

Qi – The Chinese term for the energetic components of the human being. Translate often as energy.

Saber – A cutting sword with a single edge which is generally curved. Used for slicing and slashing mainly, this weapon stands opposite of the straight sword or jian.

Shen – The spiritual, mental, and cognitive aspects of the human being. This includes conscious and sub-conscious thought. Often translated as spirit.

Simple Posture – When one takes a small portion of a longer posture and isolates a single movement as a stand alone practice or action.

Single-Lock – When the swords are engaged and one swordsman has control of the opponent's arm or sword at the hilt.

Spirit – The overarching term used when translating Shen to english. This is one of the 3 components of the human being, and includes all mental and cognitive function.

Split – In terms of foundational taiji fencing, the split is an action done with the Swordsman's Hex to divide the opponent's intention from the main engagement and bring some of their focus to your off-hand.

Stance – The position of the feet, legs, and hips. Each stance applies it's shape differently, and by connecting stances, various new intentions can be acted upon.

Static Posture – When one holds a single moment (often times the final shape) of a moving posture for an extended period of time. Holding a static posture builds strength, stability, tendons, and spirit.

Straight Sword – The english term used when discussing the Jian. This book is entirely focused on the Daoist application of the straight sword.

Strike – To attack the opponent with a slashing, piercing, or burgeoning action.

Sword – Generally refers to any long-bladed weapon which is not mounted to a pole. Specifically in taiji fencing, the sword is specifically used for the straight double-edged sword (jian). The term "saber" is applied to the curved single-edge variety in this context.

Sword Dance – When a swordsman performs a variety of connected postures and movements in continuation with one another. Often times, the term "sword dance" is reserved for un-choreographed formsets.

Sword Fight – When two people engage in combat with swords.

Sword Finger – Another term for the Swordsman's Hex. Refers to the sword in one hand, and a finger which acts as a sword in the other.

Swordplay – An umbrella term for the total sum of sword practice and cultivation skills being employed in one's skill development.

Swordsman – One that has dedicated their life or the defense of their loved ones to the sword.

Swordsman's Hex – The formal term used when discussing the shape held by the left hand when wielding a straight sword in the right hand. This position is made up by extending the index and middle finger forward, while making a large circle between the thumb and smallest two fingers. Used for combat and religious ritual.

Tai Chi – An older rendition of "taiji" from Chinese to English.

Taiheshan – The former name of the Wudang Mountains. This name translates literally as " Great Harmony Mountain."

Taiji (art) – A broad term referring to the martial arts based upon the practice of Taijiquan. All of the Taiji arts follow underlying principles which are considered one family of practices.

Taiji (term) – Referring to the state of interplay and mixing of yin and yang. This term often times refers to universal laws of balance between opposites which are mutually co-dependent.

Taiji Fencing (sport) – A formalized version of cohesion fencing which requires swordsmen to engage blades, cut, and escape without being touched by the opponent's weapon.

Taiji Fencing (practice) – A more combat oriented version of tuijian, but without the rules and points of the formal taiji fencing sport.

Taijijian – The term for Taiji arts using the jian. Often done smooth and slow, most taiji systems have a straight sword form to supplement the open-hand art.

**Taijiquan** – The formal english spelling of the popular martial art and health practice, tai chi. This martial art consists of a variety of principles relating to appropriate application of force and structure in striking and grappling combat.

**Taijitu** – The image used to describe the cosmological state of yin and yang. Often times called a yin-yang symbol in the west, the term translates more accurately to "diagram of the supreme universal principle."

**Taiyi (term)** – In Daoist cosmology, Taiyi is the state of oneness before yin and yang have emerged. This state of oneness includes the "is and isn't," the up and down, and the yin and yang in totality.

**Taiyi (art)** – A blanket term for all of the Taiyi arts practiced in the Daoist community, and made famous at the Wudang Mountains. These arts are recognized as the art from which Taiji, Bagua, and other Daoist martial arts have risen from. Prominent features include slow steady movements with surprise bursts of energy, extreme balancing and squatting postures, and a twisting winding waist.

Taiyijian – The term for the sword arts found in the Taiyi martial skill set. These forms often have a flowing continuous sword, while the swordsman twists and turns in all directions.

Taiyiquan – The term for all of the Taiyi martial arts, but referring specifically to the empty-hand practice.

Tao – The older way of writing "Dao." Used to describe both the saber and the religious term.

Taoism – The older translation of Daoism, the indigenous religion of China.

Thread – When an action is achieved by moving each joint in proportion to one another, as if threading beads along a necklace.

Threat – When one swordsman's blade has a clear line of attack on their opponent.

Three Treasures – These three treasures are the three components of the human being. The physical being Jing, the energetic being Qi, and the spiritual/mental being Shen.

Throw – To toss or project an object or weapon at an opponent or target.

Tip – The part of the sword with angled edges merging into a point. Also known as the "leaf."

Tuijian – The practice of developing sensitivity in the engagement by pushing swords back and forth. Literally translated as, "push swords."

Tuishou – The practice of developing sensitivity in empty-handed combat for striking and grappling. Literally translated as, "push hands."

Wooden Sword – A practice sword designed to emulate the balance and weight of a real sword for use in training and fencing.

Wu-Tang – An older translation of Wudang.

Wudang (arts) – This term has two definitions. In the broader (less accurate) use, Wudang may refer to any internal art as they are said to be transmitted through Daoism initially. The more accurate term refers to any martial art specifically passed across the Daoist community, and often times preserved at Wudang Mountain.

Wudang (mountain) – The holy mountain of Daoist martial arts in China. This mountain's name refers to the patron deity of the mountain, Zhenwu, The

Perfected Warrior. Formally known as Taihe Mountain.

Wuji – The state of the universe before anything can be defined or discussed. Wuji is often translated as the empty chaos or the void before creation.

Wuwei – Referred to in the Daoist scripture of the *Zhuangzi*, this term often times is used in fencing when discussing reactive actions and responsive techniques. It is also used when discussing having a carefree attitude or the ability to let go of being fixed to change and fit the circumstances as needed.

Wushu (term) – Literally translated as "martial art," this term can be applied to any martial art, and specifically Chinese.

Wushu (sport) – The formal sport wushu is a performance competition revolving around the practice of specific formsets and choreography. These forms are designed more for aesthetic and difficulty, than function and combat application.

Wuxue – The traditional Daoist term the,"martial studies." Similar to the term wushu, wuxue implies one is studying not expressing.

Xingyi – A shorthand term for the Xingyiquan arts.

Xingyijian – The sword arts practiced in conjuncture with Xingyiquan, and utilizing the principles and shapes developed within.

Xingyiquan – Xingyiquan is an open-handed martial art practiced in the Daoist community. This skill is thought to be a Chinese-Muslim art which was later adopted by the Daoists and modified to fit the cosmology of the religion.

Yang (term) – Often used in contrast with *yin*, Yang refers to the active component in any action. In terms of fencing, we define yang as the creative force in any given moment.

Yijing – One of the oldest written text in the world, the Yijing offers insight into how things evolve and change around us. Through the study of the Yijing, it is said that "all will be revealed."

Yin – The passive component to Taiji, yin is the listening or responsive action being changed by the Yang force. If one is being responsive, they are yin to the opponent's creativity.

Yiquan – A martial art derived from the internal practices (including taijiquan and xingyiquan), This martial art focuses on having the right internal structures and body alignment, over any specific forms, postures, or techniques.

Zhang Sanfeng – The Wudang priest thought to have created Taijiquan from a dream. Also translated as Chang San Feng.

Zhanzhuang – Translated as, "standing like a post," these practices include any static posture holding methods. These are used to develop and strengthen the tendons and small muscle groups throughout the body.

Zhuangzi – Daoist sage from ~350 B.C. credited for writing the first text on sword strategy and practicing reactiveness in life.

FOR MORE BOOKS IN THE SERIES, DETAILS ON UPCOMING EVENTS & WORKSHOPS, & ONLINE TRAINING MATERIAL, PLEASE VISIT THE WEBSITE AT

**WWW.DAOISTSWORD.COM**

Printed in Great Britain
by Amazon